DATE DUE

'81

DEMCO

THE WOMAN EXECUTIVE

THE WOMAN EXECUTIVE

by Evelyn H. Park

shley books inc •
Box 768 • Port Washington, N. Y. 11050

Published simultaneously in Canada by George J. McLeod, Limited, 73 Bathurst Street, Toronto, Ontario M5V 2P8

THE WOMAN EXECUTIVE
© Copyright by Dr. Evelyn H. Park

Library of Congress Number: 77-80278
ISBN: 0-87949-086-1

Address information to Ashley Books, Inc., Box 768, Port Washington, New York 11050

Published by Ashley Books, Inc.
Manufactured in the United States of America

First Edition

9 8 7 6 5 4 3 2 1

TO
MY HUSBAND, WILFORD

THE WOMAN EXECUTIVE

CHAPTER ONE

Eve sat in the corner of the busy cafeteria where she came almost every noon, eating her lunch. The tables around her were filling rapidly, this being the time of day when office buildings in the downtown area spewed their inhabitants by the thousands into the streets. The all too few eating places were quickly filled with long queues of people waiting for tables at restaurants or for a place in the cafeteria lines. Eve usually tried to leave her office early to avoid waiting too long. The tempo of speed and restlessness pervaded everywhere and the lunch hour was not usually a time of peace and quiet, rather one of eating quickly and leaving as soon as possible in order to vacate a table for the next person.

Today Eve was deep in thought, completely oblivious to the hum of voices around her which rose to an ever-higher crescendo. She seemed isolated, her surroundings not penetrating her innermost being. She had come to a crossroad in her life, and would have to make a decision soon which fork in the road she would take. It was a fairly common occurrence among women who, like Eve, combined a career with marriage, although the husbands' interests were at stake and contrary to their own ambitions. There was a gnawing feeling inside her and the food she was trying to swallow seemed to catch in her throat. She was trying desperately to pull herself together to face the responsibilities that still lay ahead of her, and to push her own troubled thoughts into the background.

The day had started with an early morning radio announcement of the freezing drizzle that was turning the roads into a nightmare, and warning motorists to take it easy, drive slowly and cautiously on the slippery streets. Eve had dreaded the ride to work. The going would be slow, there would be stalled cars and many bumped fenders. Her spirits dropped even before she got out of bed. Shared misery would have made it much easier to bear. Until a few months ago she had shared the ride to and from work with her husband, Ed Wood. But he was now semi-retired, and only went to work when he felt like it. Today he preferred to stay

11

home with a good book to read. She mulled over the events of the morning at the office. It seemed this was just not her day. She should have turned over when she heard the weather forecast, and stayed in bed. But she could not turn her back on the responsibilities she had so willingly accepted many years ago. Neither could she hide from them. As far as her career was concerned, her private life took a back seat. That is, until she reached the present impasse. She loved the challenges that came with her job, and though there were problems, they were not insurmountable. She felt exhilarated every time she had new programs to plan. She was the administrator of a large public health program providing health services to mothers and children of poor and near-poor families. Her position brought her prestige, but she also derived genuine satisfaction from the knowledge that her job was in keeping with her need to help other people. Eve had a strange mixture of pride and humility in her make-up. She also had great ambition. Her heritage had been that she could do anything she set her mind to. Her maternal grandmother had taught Eve that no person was superior to herself, regardless of money and position, and that she should bow to no one. The humility probably came from her father. She had grown up in a religious home, and from the beginning was made aware that her life's work should be in service to others. That she was a girl made no difference to her parents as far as her future career plans were concerned, and she had their support all through medical school.

Eve's mind jerked back to today. One of the least desirable aspects of her job had to do with personnel problems. This morning she had attended a conference with the personnel director of the agency and with one of her supervisors, regarding the firing of an aide. Eve found it distasteful to fire anyone, even with reason to do so, as in this case. The aide was a woman in her middle fifties, still in the first six months of probationary employment. She had come to America as a young adult, and had never been able to shed the authoritarian, rigid culture of her past. She had previously worked on an assembly line in a factory. This in itself had made it difficult for her to adjust to her present job. Much worse was her judgemental attitude toward the patients, and her strong disapproval of the lifestyle of some of them. She

12

herself led an exemplary life and was a hard worker. Her supervisor had tried to stress to her that she was not to criticize the patients for things she did not approve of, but she persisted in her attitudes. She also felt and showed the patients that their misfortunes were their own fault and she had no compassion for their problems. New employees generally needed help in understanding those they were to serve, many of whom had very different lifestyles, customs and mores from themselves. But they honestly tried to change their outlook and accept the patients as they were without imposing their own values on them. After a period of time they were at least partially successful in being able to overcome their own prejudices.

In recent months there had been rumblings about the arrogance and authoritarian ways of the "establishment" in general, and Eve could not allow any employee of hers to provide justification for such criticism. The minority races were especially sensitive about intentional and unintentional slights and discourtesies, and made their grievances known to the Civil Rights Commission. There was always the possibility of such a complaint in Eve's department, because a large portion of the patients were black or American Indian. Since the employee in question was still in her probationary period she could be discharged without further ado, but the woman was putting up a big fight which resulted in the unusual conference with the personnel officer. It had been suggested to the woman that she resign voluntarily so she would have no blemish on her employment record, but she vehemently refused to do so. She had complained bitterly, first to Eve and then to the personnel officer, about the shabby treatment she had received from her supervisor. She discussed her problem loudly in the employees' lunchroom, cornering every person who would listen to her. The situation had become untenable. Her accusations were beginning to divide the department into those few who sided with her and were threatening to resign in protest with her, and the others who felt she was wrong.

Her supervisor had reviewed her evaluation report this morning with Eve and the personnel officer. It had been previously discussed with the aide at Eve's request. There was no way that she could be retained. If she were allowed to stay she would only cause further trouble. The decision of the firing was upheld. Eve felt no satisfaction over the decision; rather it depressed her even more and she felt somehow that she herself had failed. She was sorry for the woman. She knew that it would be difficult for her to get another job at her age. She could not expect a recommendation from Eve's agency. In short, she had probably lost her livelihood. But Eve had to concede that the woman had brought about her own misfortune, as she so often had criticized the patients of doing.

There had also been another confrontation of a completely different nature that morning. Eve had been the arbiter in a power struggle among her brightest and most ambitious young staff members. They were all specialists in their fields, and served as consultants to other staff. They all had the best interests of the patients at heart but were protective of their own professional competence. They were aggressive and could not accept suggestions from their peers. This type of confrontation was something Eve expected. She considered it a challenge to meld them together harmoniously, without any one of them losing his identity. She had tried to get them to consider their own strengths and weaknesses, and knew from experience how difficult it was for them to accept. Eve had stressed to the group that the main objective was quality service to the patients, and they should forget their rivalries and concentrate instead on what contribution each could best make to achieve this goal. She chuckled now, even as she was rubbing her aching forehead. It was the very earnestness of her staff, who though they had so much to learn yet, possessed the qualities that would make everything turn out all right in the end. Some progress had already been made. One of the group reluctantly had admitted, "I know we can't work together as long as we are angry at one another. It would probably be better to wait a little while, so let's sit on it and get together after a few days when we can look at things more calmly and objectively."

As they were leaving Eve's office, this same young woman had whispered into Eve's ear, "You know I kind of like those two others when I'm not angry at them," to which Eve had replied, "O. K., then be angry less often!" at which the other had left the room with a sheepish grin.

As Eve went over this occurrence, her turbulent thoughts receded and the deep furrows on her forehead smoothed

14

out. She could look at things in their proper perspective again. That was what made her job so interesting and even sometimes thrilling. Her spirits rose for a moment, until her thoughts returned to her personal problems. She didn't want to change one iota of the life she was now living, and yet. . . .

It had been slightly less than two decades ago, but Eve remembered it as though it had happened yesterday. She was an aspiring young physician eager to climb the ladder to greater things, but still at the beck and call of her seniors. She felt something was missing in her life in spite of her good position. In the evenings after work, she came home to an empty apartment and there was no one there to whom she could talk of her successes nor on whose shoulder she could cry when things went wrong. At times she became so depressed she felt there was nothing more to look forward to in her life. Becoming a successful professional woman did not seem sufficient for a well-rounded life. Something additional was needed.

Then it happened. Eve was sitting at a long table behind a screen in the large auditorium where a polio clinic was being conducted, sipping her coffee and enjoying the break from the bustle beyond the screen. From the beginning, she had been involved in the planning of this program with others in the agency. Now, as a physician, she was working at the public clinic she had helped plan, administering the newly discovered polio vaccine to the thousands of youngsters-that came. One of the agency nurses was sitting nearby, also enjoying the coffee break.

A third person entered. He was another physician in the agency, somewhat older than Eve and with whom she had had some dealings. She did not really know much about him, except that he was a widower. He sat down with his cup and looked around, saying something like, "It's nice to rest for a while." There was silence until suddenly to Eve's surprise, as the nurse left the table to fill her coffee cup again from the urn a few steps away, the newcomer quietly asked Eve if she would like to have dinner with him that evening. Eve could hardly believe her ears. She replied, equally quietly, "I'd like to, if it can be early enough so I can get to an eight o'clock meeting."

That was how it began. Even on her first date with Ed,

15

Eve Hart's career was paramount and had been, ever after. She was always a career woman first and a wife second. There were difficulties in adjustment at first. In addition to a husband, she also inherited his teen-aged and younger sons. Gradually the difficulties subsided. The boys, one by one, left home for college and their careers, and Eve and Ed were left alone. Life became so peaceful that Eve was moved to exclaim, "This is almost like paradise!" At the same time her career began to soar and she gratefully acknowledged to Ed that he was to a large extent responsible for it. Her happiness made her more confident and she could now share her successes as well as disappointments with him. His quiet manner of listening to her, interspersed with appropriate comments, resulted in her being able to look at matters in their proper prospective and enabled her to make sounder decisions.

As life went on, it brought changes, ever so subtle at first. Immediately following Ed's partial retirement, it didn't seem to make much difference to either of them that he now stayed at home most of the time. They still had each other in the evenings and weekends. When Ed had worked full time their contacts were limited to various meetings they attended, and as often as possible, they tried to have lunch together. It wasn't easy to pinpoint how and when the change started. Previously they had shared the ride to and from work, and rehashed the events of the day, and unless some major happenings had occurred, by the time they reached home the affairs of the office were behind them, and they could enjoy their home life together. Now Eve found herself sharing less and less with Ed. In the short time Ed had been away, so much occurred at the agency that it was difficult for Eve to discuss her concerns with Ed. It was necessary for her to provide a lot of background information before he understood what she was talking about, with the result that she told him less and less. She began to feel very much alone again. She had a vague feeling that perhaps she and Ed were pulling apart. Though Ed never mentioned it, he didn't seem altogether happy with her total commitment to her career. Was it possible that they had begun to live side by side but separately? Where and how would it end?

Eve looked at her watch. Had she really been here so long? She finished her hamburger which was now cold, and started on her apple pie. Although she was far from happy, her moment of solitude had brought some measure of relief to her turbulent thoughts and helped her to gain back at least a superficial composure. She pushed her problems to the back of her consciousness and prepared to return to the office. She walked back slowly. The sky was still gray and overcast, but the drizzle had stopped and the streets were no longer slippery, only wet and slushy. The approaching Christmas season brought the Salvation Army pots to the street corners and bells were jingling in the air, calling for donations for gifts for the poor. Loud-speakers in the bus shelters in the middle of each block blasted the familiar Christmas carols while people hurried on their way, many loaded with packages. It seemed to Eve that the message of good cheer was not reflected on their faces; rather they seemed for the most part tense and withdrawn, never glancing at others on the street. She trudged along in the slush until she reached her office. Any thoughts she might have had of the approaching Christmas season receded from her mind as she immediately became involved in staff conferences and matters requiring her complete attention.

CHAPTER TWO

·The daylight hours were becoming ever shorter as Christmas approached. After the busy weekdays, Eve loved and appreciated her weekends. But now, since it was so close to Christmas, even these were work-filled. She carefully scheduled her activities on Saturdays so as to complete the home tasks that were necessary to keep up the family traditions at Christmas. With great effort she decided to forget her personal problems for the time being, and concentrate on more immediate concerns. The first of these was the baking of a delicious, prune-filled, star-shaped pastry, from the heritage of her childhood. She remembered with longing those years of long ago, when the house was filled with the delicious odors of cooking and baking for days and even weeks before Christmas. In no way could Eve compete with her mother's preparations. She had neither the time nor the inclination to bake. Fortunately she could buy most things, especially the cakes and cookies which were considered a part of the Christmas season. Eve also anticipated receiving a box of homemade cookies, as she did each year after the office Christmas party in her department. Several of her staff were excellent cooks and enjoyed showing off their creations at the party.

The Saturdays sped by all too quickly, as Eve and Ed prepared for the approaching holiday season. The tree had been bought, brought in and decorated, and was now standing in all its glory in the living room. On Christmas Eve, the snow fell gently. It would be a white Christmas. It was the darkest time of the year, but the white snow and the colored lights on the tree made for light and joy. The radio softly played the Christmas carols that sounded so right, in contrast to the blaring from the loud-speakers downtown.

A delicious smell permeated the house. Eve was in the midst of the final preparations for the Christmas Eve dinner which would be in the tradition of her background, while tomorrow's meal would follow Ed's traditions. She felt happy and contented, and warm inside. Everything was as it used to be. Ed helped her by setting the table and doing those other chores she gave him. He seemed happy to do them. His moods seemed very dependent on how Eve felt. When she was depressed or remote from him, he seemed to draw into himself too, and there would be a tense look on his face. Recently this had happened all too often, but now all was well. They were far removed from everything that troubled them. They gave each other their full attention and their love could almost be felt.

For the first few years after their marriage, and while their sons were still at home, they had had a full-time housekeeper. They had no other choice, since Eve could not have managed both home and her career. But after the boys left home, they managed well with part-time help. Ed helped with so many chores, and they each had their own special tasks. Eve's responsibility was mainly the cooking. At first, Ed had puttered around the kitchen, but this had irritated Eve until she finally told him, "If you feel that I can't handle the cooking by myself, I will be more than happy to leave it to you, and get out of the kitchen myself." Ed had only meant to be helpful, and was perfectly happy to leave the cooking to her.

For this Christmas Eve they invited a colleague who had been widowed three months earlier, and her two teenage sons to share the dinner with them. They felt that Maggie and her sons would feel their loss less acutely with them. Eve set the table festively, even using the Santa centerpiece that came from the days when she was still single. They had barely finished dressing for the gala evening when the doorbell rang and there were Maggie and the two boys.

Soon all were seated at the table with the candles glowing softly and their light flickering on their faces. They bowed their heads as Ed asked for the blessing on all. The food was done to perfection, with Ed among the first to compliment Eve on it. In no time at all, it seemed, hungry appetites of young and old alike were appeased. The boys were quiet and almost too well-behaved. Their upbringing showed in their courtesy to their elders, but Eve felt that their recent loss and sorrow subdued them and showed in their sad eyes.

After dinner they all went into the living room, where the lovely spruce stood in the corner. It was decorated with the usual baubles and colored lights with a tinsel star at its top almost touching the ceiling. Ed picked up the Bible from a side table and asked the group to listen as he read the old story of Christmas just as Eve's father had done so long ago. After Ed finished, Eve asked, "Would you like to sing some Christmas carols with us now?" Maggie replied they could try, adding with a chuckle, "None of us have good voices, but we'll do our best."

The voices of the boys were a bit husky, Ed's was a bit off key and Maggie's and Eve's sopranos were rather weak, as they sang the carols to Eve's accompaniment at the piano. The group would never have won any prizes with their singing, but they were filled with the awe of the Christmas spirit, and they all sang happily.

After their guests departed, and Eve and Ed had cleared the table, they went back into the darkened living room where all the lights were out, with the exception of those on the tree. They sat close to each other on the couch holding hands, as with misty eyes they watched and listened to the Swedish angel bells twinkling and twirling around the lighted candles. The air was filled with peace and love, their love for each other and for the gift of Christmas. Late Christmas Eve had been a time Eve and Ed had devoted to each other during their entire married life. It was a precious time for them, a time for reflection and renewal of spirit, an oasis in their busy lives. This was also the time they exchanged their gifts. Ed often gave Eve a piece of jewelry. He had exquisite taste and his gifts pleased Eve greatly.

Eve awoke on Christmas morning, looked at the bedside clock and saw that it was only 7:30. There was no point in getting up. It was still dark outside and there were no young children in the house eager to get to stockings hung in front of the fireplace. It was blissful to luxuriate a while between sleep and full wakefulness. Wakefulness finally won over sleep. It was about time to get up anyway. Ed would want to get started with the turkey and the dressing. Even though Eve did the cooking, when the time came for fixing the turkey once or twice a year, by unspoken agreement Ed was the one who did it. Besides, turkey at Christmas was a part of Ed's tradition which they followed on Christmas Day. Ed wanted all the elbow room he could muster, and besides, he didn't want Eve, a stickler for order, complaining about the mess he made all over the kitchen. Not until the turkey was in the oven and he had cleaned up, was she allowed to enter the kitchen to prepare breakfast, and the rest of the dinner.

Today their three unmarried sons would come for dinner and spend the rest of the day and evening with them.

The dining room table was as on the evening before. The same Christmas tablecloth covered the table and Eve's old Santa in his sleigh, surrounded by his reindeer, adorned the center of the table. The young men were so large, and seemed to fill the table so completely, that Eve and Ed felt dwarfed in their presence. It was a noisy group as the brothers joshed and teased each other. There were exclamations of praise for Ed's masterpiece as he carried in the golden brown turkey. The mashed potatoes were white and fluffy — always Ed's job to mash — and the cranberries, yams and jello salad gave color to the table amidst the other foods. Ed skillfully carved the turkey. It was a joy to watch him do it with hands that at one time had performed surgery. Oh, how the young men ate, doing justice to the delicious offerings and consuming gallons of milk to wash down all the food. After the main course, the traditional plum pudding and sauce followed. Everything tasted so good. The sons finally decided they had had enough and went into the living room, leaving the ravaged table to Ed and Eve. Eve was ready to drop from fatigue.

"Why don't you go and rest for awhile? I'll get the boys to help," Ed suggested.

"You must be as tired as I am," Eve remonstrated.

"I'll rest later," he replied, and went into the living room to corral his reluctant sons to help him.

They were soon finished and gathered once more in the living room. It was time for more Christmas carols and then, finally, the presents. The youngest son usually had the pleasant task of playing Santa Claus and bringing out the gifts, one at a time, from under the tree. Everyone seemed satisfied and happy with his gifts, and soon it was time to eat again! This time it was to taste Eve's Christmas tarts and other baked goodies. At last, Eve and Ed were alone. It was late. The day had been a happy one with hustle and bustle, but quite different from the mood of the evening before, with its more simple offerings and greater emphasis on the religious meaning of Christmas.

Eve stayed home the day after Christmas. She appeared bleary-eyed at the breakfast table, and was aghast at the weight gain the scale had showed that morning. She needed a cup of coffee to get going, and then a brisk walk outdoors. They both bundled up in their warm winter jackets, boots, caps and mittens to brave the cold. The trees in the park across the street were white with frost that sparkled in the sunshine. As usual, when the weather was cold, Eve began walking briskly and called to Ed, "This will make my blood circulate!"

"Slow down, I can't keep up with you. It's not good for me to rush like this in the cold," Ed replied.

"I always forget. But I get cold when I walk too slowly," Eve said, as she began to match her steps to Ed's. She was well aware that it was dangerous for him to over-exert himself in cold weather because of a heart condition. She felt guilty that again she had forgotten, and blamed herself for forcing Ed to remain in this cold climate when he would have felt so much better elsewhere. But she was not yet ready to sacrifice her career to accomplish this. Her mood went down a few degrees but improved as they walked along. Their cheeks soon became red from the cold, and their breath showed in the air. Children with new sleds were having fun sliding down the slopes of the lawns in front of their homes and in the park. There was much laughter and shouting. Someone had built a huge snowman in the park, complete with stocking cap and scarf. Dogs mingled with the children and got in the way of their sledding. A dog or two ran ahead of his owner who was pulling him back from his explorations as he darted to every tree along the way. The snow crunched underfoot as Eve and Ed walked on. Every once in a while they stopped to watch the children. They could have continued walking indefinitely but for the cold nipping at their noses and bringing tears to their eyes. Reluctantly they turned and proceeded homeward. As they opened the back door, the fragrant smell of their breakfast coffee greeted them, seeming to say, "Welcome back."

After a light lunch, they settled down to reading the newspapers and browsing through their new gift books. But soon Eve could hardly keep her eyes open and began yawning.

"Time for your nap," said Ed and went upstairs for a pillow and a light cover for Eve. She lay down on the couch in the living room and Ed tucked the cover around her. "Have a nice sleep, sweetheart. I'll go upstairs to finish reading the papers, so you can sleep in peace." And so Eve drifted off to sleep. After half an hour, she awakened but lay still for a few more minutes as consciousness gradually returned. Oh, what a deep, sweet sleep she had had. She got up, folded the blanket and carried it and the pillow upstairs. She glanced into the room where Ed had gone to read the papers. As usual, wearied of reading he had drifted off to sleep just when Eve was through with her nap. "Oh, well, let the poor dear enjoy his sleep now," she said.

It was gradually growing dark. Eve plugged in the lights on the Christmas tree and turned on the record player for some soft music as she curled up in the corner of the couch to listen. Soon Ed came downstairs refreshed from his sleep, to join her, and the peaceful atmosphere of Christmas continued.

The short holiday had spiritually renewed Eve and she could again think of returning tomorrow to her everyday world to meet whatever challenges it brought with it. Her personal decision could be delayed for a while yet.

CHAPTER THREE

Christmas over, winter set in with a vengeance. The weatherman warned of a drop in temperatures which were already near zero. There was no question of Ed venturing out into the cold for their customary before-dinner walk. Even Eve, though well bundled up, felt the cold so intensely that she had to cut her walk short before she reached the end of the block. After dinner they settled down in the living room with their newspapers, but felt a chill near the windows. Their house was usually snug, but when a brisk wind blew from the north, combined with sub-zero temperatures, it felt chilly. They decided it would be more comfortable upstairs, so they moved up.

Ed was not in his usual good mood. He felt trapped at having to stay alone indoors for so long.

"I can't see how you still think it's so wonderful staying up here in the frozen north. If you wait much longer, you won't have me around to enjoy things when you finally decide to cut loose from your job." He had now brought his dissatisfaction out into the open.

"Well, you can't just suddenly make me leave everything. I have so many unfinished projects, and besides, I can't even get a pension yet!"

"Suit yourself!" grumbled Ed as he buried his head in the newspaper. The rest of the evening was spent with no conversation between them, each in his own thoughts, Ed feeling sorry for himself, and Eve torn with indecision. On the one hand, she felt for Ed and his constricted lifestyle. On the other hand, she was determined to stay on and see the fruit of her labors for which she had struggled so long. The financial considerations were also important to her. Before they went to bed, Eve promised Ed, "As soon as I can arrange it, I'll try to take time off so we can go south on a vacation. I can take the major portion of my annual leave in the winter, but I'd like to have a week free for the summer too. Actually I can stand the cold better than the awful heat."

"Well, I can't," retorted Ed.

"Please, don't be so grouchy. You're making it awfully

hard for me," begged Eve. "I think we could leave in a month's time. Why don't you study travel brochures and decide where we should go?"

"I suppose that's better than nothing. I hope by the time we get back, it won't be too long before we have spring."

During the night Eve was awakened by sounds in the corners of the house, and had trouble falling asleep again. At other times she would roll over into Ed's arms and in no time was asleep again. But this time she had no desire to awaken him, because he had still been in a bad mood when they went to bed, although the thought of the winter vacation had made him feel a little better. Her thoughts went back to the time when they decided to get married. There had been no question but that Eve would continue to work. There would be no children to interfere with her career and she would maintain her own name since she had already established herself professionally as Dr. Hart. Ed had supported her in all these decisions. They had also considered the time when Ed would retire which would occur several years before she did. This did not loom as a problem at the time because it would be many, many years hence. They had agreed that Eve would continue to work until she had accumulated sufficient years of service to earn a pension for herself, but no longer.

Ed had stood up to his end of the verbal agreement and soon Eve could take early retirement. Ed had been able to continue working beyond his usual retirement age, thus shortening the interval until Eve's possible retirement. Cutting down to part-time work a few months ago had been mutually agreed upon by Ed and the agency. His responsibilities had made Ed very tense during the last months of his full employment, and were taking a toll on his health. Eve was happy when the decision to ease up was made. Ed had felt so much better, and his tensions had disappeared. But now he could not stand his enforced idleness. He was becoming very impatient just sitting at home. Besides escaping the cold in the winter, he wanted to travel more than they could with Eve so tied up.

Eve grew more and more restless and began to toss and turn. She gave full credit to Ed for helping her to achieve her position. Her career was at its peak. How could she chuck everything now? She could continue for a number of years and she still had ambitions to pursue. She could not decide what was more important to her right now, to continue her career or her marriage. Her tormented thoughts concluded that at this point, her career had the upper hand and only a catastrophe could make her change her mind. Her thoughts grew hazier and hazier, until at last she fell into a troubled sleep.

In the morning, the windows were frosty and the temperature registered twenty below zero. They were silent at breakfast, though just as Eve was about to leave, Ed showed concern for her and inquired if she were dressed warmly enough for the weather. She assured him she was. She had no trouble starting the car in the heated garage at home, but since she parked in an open ramp at work, it was necessary for her to leave the office a couple of times during the day to start it and let it run for a short time so it would turn over at the end of the day. The morning passed quickly. There were no great problems to deal with, for which Eve was glad, since she felt the effects of her sleepless night. When she returned from lunch, Bertha, her secretary, told her, "There are two women waiting to see you."

"That's fine. Our meeting isn't supposed to start for another fifteen minutes. We'll wait for the others to arrive before I call them in," Eve replied. Shortly Gail Hanson, the chief social worker for the clinics; Jane Johnson, a nursing supervisor; and Vincent Rice, the public relations expert arrived. Eve asked Bertha to invite the guests in. They had in the meantime been joined by two other women and a small child.

"Please take a seat around the table and make yourselves comfortable," Eve invited. The spokeswoman for the group spoke up. "As I told you over the telephone when I asked for this meeting, we're not happy that your clinics are not doing abortions, nor even referring girls for this."

"I think we should all introduce ourselves first," suggested Eve. She introduced herself and the staff members. She then waited for the visitors to give their names. One after another gave her first name. Eve inquired about their last names. The spokeswoman replied, "I don't think there is really any need for our last names. If you want to reach us you can ask for Lola at this telephone number," and handed Eve a slip of paper with a number on it. The staff looked at each other and Eve thought, "So that's the way it is. You haven't the guts to stand behind your own names."

"Have it your way," she said aloud.

"We think your birth control clinics are O. K. The girls say they're getting good care, and the doctors and nurses and all treat them nice," the spokeswoman began. "I myself think the pill is for the birds, it just isn't safe. But that's beside the point now. The girls are complaining that you discourage abortions and never refer any girls for it."

"But our state is only now considering the matter and hasn't passed a law permitting it yet, so if we did refer anybody for abortion it would be illegal," countered Gail.

"See what I mean with your holier than thou attitude? You can stay within the law and still help the girls. We aren't telling you to have the abortions done in this state."

"What are you suggesting?" asked Vincent quietly.

The woman looked at him gratefully. "You know as well as we do that many girls are having abortions done by quacks and you also know how unsafe that is. Any hospital can tell of girls coming there afterward with bleeding or infections. I don't know of any deaths, but even that could happen. We believe every woman should have the right to decide whether she wants to go through with her pregnancy or not, but in a safe way. We're pushing for women's rights."

"We're all for women's rights," said Eve.

"You're the establishment," said the woman. "We want to facilitate the referrals for abortion and to give the girls counseling."

"Where would you refer them?" asked Jane.

"We want you to send the girls to us first. Tell them that we will help them. We will then counsel them and make arrangements for them to get to an out of state clinic for abortion."

"What kind of counseling do you do, and how are your counselors trained?" asked Gail.

"We train ourselves. We tell the girls about the clinic, what it costs, how the abortion is done and then we help them make arrangements to get there."

"What do you do after the abortion for those who have problems?" asked Jane.

"They haven't had any problems."

"Oh, yes, there are problems for some after abortion,"

Gail said. "We've had girls come to us after an abortion who had terrible guilt feelings. Usually we've been able to work out the problems with them, but we had to send one girl to the mental health clinic, she was so disturbed."

The woman did not reply, but went on, "The girls that we refer must have a medical report with them and since we don't have any doctors, we can't give them a medical examination."

"So you want us to do these medical examinations before the abortion. That would still be illegal for us to do," said Eve.

"Every woman should have control over her own body and decide for herself what she wants to do in case of pregnancy. As Vincent knows, we're on the consumers' committee for your clinics, and we want to be heard regarding our rights as women. Your job is to serve us, and not the other way around. We're going to take a good hard look at all your services to see if you're short-changing us in other areas."

"Are you threatening us?" asked Eve.

"I wouldn't say that, but I think we could come up with some kind of solution that would satisfy all of us."

"I'm not so sure of that," said Eve. "Please excuse me for a minute."

The child was getting very restless, tugging at her mother, and whining. Eve went out to Bertha to get some paper and crayons. She also used this as an excuse to get ot of the room for a while. The air in the room had become very stuffy. She would have opened a window if it hadn't been so dreadfully cold outside. She came back into the room and handed the paper and crayons to the child, who soon was pushing the crayons on the paper with obvious delight. The meeting continued.

"Do you tell the girls you are sending off for abortions that after the abortion they should go on birth control?" asked Jane.

"No, we don't think that is necessary," replied one of the other women.

"You would rather have abortion after abortion," retorted Eve. "Because of the illegality of the whole thing, I don't think any of our physicians would cooperate with you."

"Aren't some doctors already referring girls for abortions

from their own offices?"

"I wouldn't know. I do agree with you on one point," said Eve. "I believe in abortions for girls who have become victims of rape or incest, such as we occasionally see in our maternity clinics."

"We're not interested in the very young girls, because the clinic won't do anything for them unless they are accompanied by a parent. We will work only with the older girls and women," said the spokeswoman.

"I can't give you any answer now," said Eve. "I have to talk it over with my staff first, and also with my boss. Whatever we do has to be within the law, especially since we are a governmental agency."

"We have to go now anyway. I'll get in touch with you next week at the latest," concluded the spokeswoman. "You can also call me at the number I gave you."

They left the room. Eve was almost overcome by the smell of body odors, sweat and even urine, probably from the child. Her head was throbbing and she felt faint. She told her staff, "Let's review all this tomorrow. After sleeping on it we will have a clearer idea of what to do. Bring me your ideas. Bertha will set up a time for us to meet."

She shivered as she started driving home at the end of the day. Her fingers were stinging with the cold and her glasses steamed up so she could hardly see. Eventually the car warmed up and driving was easier.

She thought about the afternoon's meeting; not about the issue of abortion, but that women were fighting for equal rights in so many different ways. Some denied their femininity and adopted the ways of men, others seemed to despise men and belittled them. Still others threw all modesty to the winds demeaning their sexuality, believing everything had to be as natural as the Lord had made them, wearing tight sweaters with apparently nothing between the flesh and the sweater. This in spite of the fact that they complained of the commercial exploitation made of them displaying their bodies. Eve was old-fashioned enough to feel ashamed of what these women were doing to her sex. Then there were women like the ones today, who distrusted and showed hostility toward other women who didn't agree with them. Her anger arose again as she recalled the afternoon. She certainly didn't want them to speak for her. There were any number of successful women attorneys, business women, physicians, artists and teachers who were fine examples of liberated women. Eve felt very strongly about women's rights, but at the same time she wasn't about to deny her own femininity or to put down men.

She had always given credit to her father for having really liberated her. She recalled how she had been encouraged by her parents to pursue the medical career she had chosen at the ripe old age of ten. Her decision had been instantaneous. She had been walking out of her father's study one day and as she started to go down the stairs, she announced, "I'm going to be a doctor." She had never seriously thought of any other vocation. It seemed strange to Eve now that she had stuck to this decision. She had been a rather sickly child, terrified of dentists and physicians. In later years she laughed and told how she never had prescribed castor oil to anybody because of having had castor oil mixed with orange juice poured down her throat while the doctor held her nose. She had gotten even with him though by spitting out the whole ugly mess at him!

Her first encounter with sex prejudice had come from one of her uncles who was a physician. When he heard that she was applying to medical school he had written an urgent letter to her father telling him it would be a serious mistake. He said the studies would be much too strenuous for a girl; that she would soon marry and give up her studies and in the meantime would have deprived a deserving man of a seat in medical school. He had finished the letter with, "For goodness sake don't allow her to study medicine." Even now, she felt the same fury she had experienced so many years ago. The remarkable thing was that Eve's father had been very angry with his brother, and had replied to him that he would not listen to such nonsense — that if Eve wanted to go to medical school, that was up to her. All through medical school, her father encouraged her every step of the way, but at the same time admonished her not to get involved in any way that would interfere with her studies, including marriage.

She recalled also an earlier incident of prejudice. The senior high school class had been discussing their future plans. When she said she was going to become a physician, the young male teacher became very hostile, and had belit-

31

tled her in front of the class, saying she would never make it and that she had better settle for something less. Some two or three decades later, Eve met this same teacher and was able to tell him she *had* made it and was now occupying an administrative position in a health agency. He congratulated her and was obviously proud to have been her teacher.

In medical school there had been no overt prejudice and she felt she had been treated fairly. She recalled only two minor incidents. In the first lecture by the professor of internal medicine, he had warned the fledgling females to always dress decorously and never to wear low-cut dresses to class, or in dealings with patients. Another time a fellow medical student remarked that girls should enter only social and preventive medicine, but the boys should take up clinical medicine. Only in later years did discrimination really arise. A minor fact was that when she was introduced to strangers as Dr. Hart, they invariably looked around for the nearest man, extending their hand to him before they would realize their mistake.

When she married Ed, after many years as an independent career woman, she was suddenly confronted with sex discrimination of a magnitude she had never dreamed of. She remembered the time she went to buy herself a winter coat. She had charge accounts in several stores but not in this one. As she was about to pay, the saleslady suggested she open an account, so she accompanied the saleslady to the credit office. She was told, to her great surprise, that as a married woman she could not open an account in her own name, in spite of the fact that she had a well-paying job, maintained an A credit rating and had bank accounts in her own name.

In anger she told the credit clerk, "Keep your coat, I will never enter your store again and I will see to it that none of my friends do, either."

The store manager ran after her as she was rushing from the store and called out, "We will make an exception in your case!"

Many years later the same spectre of sex discrimination appeared, at a time when Eve was troubled and depressed. She had noted some symptoms which might indicate a malignancy and Ed concurred in her suspicions. Her own physician sent her to a surgeon who specialized in cases like hers and he in turn scheduled her for immediate hospitalization in order to do a biopsy. Eve had complete hospital and medical insurance in her own name, as a fringe benefit of her job. On admission to the hospital, she advised the hospital clerk of this, and to be on the safe side she also went to the business office and told them the same thing before she was whisked off to her room. The surgeon had been so certain that Eve had a malignancy, that when the first words that reached her consciousness after surgery were, "It was benign," her immediate reaction was a soft, "Oh, thank God!"

She left the hospital in three days, to continue her recuperation at home. She was still feeling weak and very depressed from the scare of cancer when the hospital statement came, addressed not to Eve, but to Dr. Ed Wood for surgery performed on his wife Mrs. Eve Wood. Not a word about Dr. Eve Hart nor her insurance coverage. Eve sent the bill back to the hospital, stating her professional name, the name of her insurance carrier and contract number. A month later the hospital sent a duplicate bill to Ed with the addition of the insurance company and contract number on the statement and a notation that the insurance company did not acknowledge the coverage for Mrs. Eve Wood.

Eve sobbed in her frustration and weakness. Her existence as a professional woman had again been completely ignored. Because of sex discrimination she was a nonentity. As a last resort, she wrote a scathing letter to the hospital administrator, with a copy to the insurance company. Four months later the matter was satisfactorily settled, but no apology made. Eve was sure that it had been the lower echelon female clerks and the girls in the admitting and business offices who had caused all the trouble. They had obviously been incapable of using independent judgment when exceptions to the routine procedures arose. Bitterly, Eve conceded that if their performance was indicative of the intelligence and brains of the female sex, then indeed women were the inferior sex and deserved to be treated as children, or chattels, or appendages of their husbands.

Eve could derive some satisfaction in that *she* had been able to buck the system of sex discrimination, at least for herself, through her persistence. Ed had supported her throughout, but she had fought her own battles.

"It isn't fair that we must fight like this for our rights.

Surely there must be an easier way to bring about change. Those of us who do stand up are labelled aggressive and bossy," she moaned.

By the time Eve reached home, she felt empathy with the women who had met in her office that day, but she felt they were fighting for women's rights in the wrong way. There was no need to discredit other women even when issues were at stake. The next day Eve and her staff found a satisfactory solution to the dilemma of abortions, which was approved by the health officer. Gail came up with the original idea and it was improved upon by the others. It was to have all patients desiring abortions to be seen first by the clinics' social workers who would determine the patients' attitudes toward their pregnancies and would then be able to present alternatives to abortion.

"Many of the single girls panic when they find out they are pregnant. They are not aware of the medical and social services available to them which can help with plans for the baby, even arranging for adoption after birth," explained Gail.

"If a girl is absolutely determined to have an abortion, and will do so regardless of us, we will examine her to see that she has no medical problems that would prove hazardous to her health in case of abortion. We should also insist that she return to us afterward, for an examination to be followed by birth control if she continues to be sexually active," summarized Eve.

Eve was satisfied that the matter had been settled, but she was wrong. A couple of days later she received a telephone call form a woman who identified herself as a member of a group against abortions. She said she had heard that the agency was going to start making referrals for abortions and that it might be involved in court cases if anything went wrong. She requested equal time to talk to the staff so they would refer all girls wanting abortions to their group so they could be talked out of it.

"I will take your suggestion into consideration. At our next in-service education session for our staff on counseling regarding the pros and cons of abortions, we will present both sides of the issue. Perhaps someone from your group would be willing to participate," Eve suggested.

This was the way many controversial issues were handled,

by compromise. Opposing groups were not always satisfied with the solution, but usually went along with it. Women themselves were on opposite sides involving women's rights. Abortion was a hot issue with religious and political overtones, but regardless of her own feelings, Eve wanted to do everything in a legal manner.

Eve was bothered for some time by the thought that there was someone in her department who had leaked information to the anti-abortion group, but lacked the courage to identify herself to her.

CHAPTER FOUR

"Breakfast is ready," Ed called up to Eve. Since his retirement, he had taken on the task of preparing the simple breakfast so the mornings would be less rushed.

"I'm on my way," Eve replied as she ran down the stairs.

"Only one more week to go and we're off to the warm southwest," she commented after she had finished her first cup of coffee and was reaching for the pot to pour herself another. "But it's going to be a busy week with all the public clinics we'll be having. We expect to vaccinate some fifty thousand children against German measles."

"Just like twenty years ago, when we worked together at the polio clinics. Only now here I sit at home, and you're in the midst of it all and barely have time to think of the vacation, much less prepare for it."

"Now, Ed, you know I'll be ready in plenty of time and we'll leave just as we planned. You're not by any chance jealous of my being in the thick of things?"

"Heaven forbid! But you know as well as I do that here I'm sitting on a limb just waiting when we could be starting a new life and getting involved in new things together."

Eve did not reply, but got up and kissed Ed on the cheek as she left the table. Her happy mood of anticipation had again been squashed and she felt guilty and unhappy. She thought to herself, "Maybe it would be better if we went our separate ways. We're just making each other miserable."

Fortunately, Eve was so busy all the next week she could push her private thoughts into the background. The planning for the clinics was completed, now the action occurred and again Eve was satisfied that the planning had been wise. Many different persons were involved and the wishes of others in the community had been met, as far as possible. There had been the principal who had refused the facilities of his school for a clinic because he didn't want his pupils to develop a distaste and fear of school by thinking that it was a place where they would be stuck with needles. The majority of school principals, on the other hand, were delighted when their school was selected as a clinic site. One spoke for all when he said, "I'm very worried about the low levels of immunization in our school. This should help greatly. I only wish you would come back later and conduct another clinic here, and give all the other shots that are necessary, such as against diphtheria."

There was already a flurry of activity going on at the office as Eve arrived. Supplies were being loaded into vans to be taken to clinics and the staff was rushing to gather up those who would ride to their different assignments. Eve had assigned herself to the clinic in the downtown headquarters. In this way she could be reached by the outlying clinics if problems arose, and at the same time be available to the nurses in her own clinic who were actually administering the vaccine according to written medical orders for which she was responsible. Eve conferred first with Bertha about routine matters that had to be taken care of, and then sauntered over to the clinic to see how things were going. As was expected, there were not very many school-age children at this downtown clinic, but a large number of preschoolers were going through the lines. The clinic was proceeding in an orderly manner. An occasional child balked when his turn came for the shot. Such a child usually spread his fears to those following him, and they all cried, but no epidemic of frightened children developed, because the balking child, once he had been convinced to go through with the ordeal, exclaimed with delighted surprise, "It didn't even hurt!"

Eve felt a warm glow as she followed this episode from the sidelines. During a short lull, she sat down with the nurses and volunteers who were helping with non-nursing functions. One of the nurses told her, "You know, your husband is one of the kindest persons I ever met. He always had time to listen to us when we were in his department, and he always gave us just the advice we needed, but he made us think things through on our own too. It was an excellent learning experience for me to have worked with him."

Just then a patient entered. The staff got up and the work went on. Bertha appeared at the door, motioning to Eve. She was wanted on the telephone. Eve took the call in her own office. It was one of the nurses in an outlying clinic. The doctor there had requested the nurse to call Eve regarding an unusual situation. Eve listened, asked a few questions and then gave her opinion. She worked at her desk for the next hour and then returned to the clinic. There was almost a festive atmosphere in the agency. It was a change from the ordinary and everybody got caught up in the excitement of dealing with thousands of people. Even though staff, including Eve, worked long into the evening, their buoyancy kept them going and they did not feel their fatigue until they went to bed, only to continue the same the next day.

The clinics continued all week. Eve did not have much time to even talk to Ed, much less to determine what his mood was. On Friday afternoon when everything was over, the results were tabulated. The initial estimate of some fifty thousand vaccinations was fairly accurate. Eve breathed a sigh of relief. The program had been successful, and well worth the time and effort expended.

"Now the children will be protected and their unborn siblings along with them," Eve told her staff. "The children will not bring the disease home to the mother and even if she should be pregnant in the first three months, there will be no danger to her unborn child, who otherwise might be born with abnormalities if his mother had contacted the German measles."

She thanked all who had participated in the program. After making final plans with her assistant for coverage during her vacation, Eve cleared her desk and left the office behind her as she went home to pack for their trip which would start tomorrow. The cold weather continued and she was glad she could leave for a warmer climate for herself and especially on Ed's account. She was determined not to let anything interfere with their enjoyment of the vacation. She hoped that Ed would feel likewise. He had chosen the southwest deserts for their vacation because it was a place they had never visited. Each year they selected a different place, each with the common ingredients of sun, warmth and water. Neither Ed nor Eve was a great athlete but they did enjoy swimming, sunning themselves, loafing, reading, walking for exercise and sightseeing.

Ed had collected books, maps and brochures to find out about the topography, the scenic attractions, the people and the weather. He had even made a preliminary plan of side-trips. He shared his findings and tentative plans with Eve as they drove along. They left at dawn on Saturday. They were aware of the hazards of winter driving, so they loaded the trunk of their car with plenty of blankets, heavy clothing and food supplies in case they got stranded, as well as the lighter clothes they hoped to wear later on. Their car purred contentedly and seemed as eager as its owners to be on its way. Eve and Ed took turns driving.

At the end of each day they pulled in at motels in time for dinner. Ed wanted to get going early each morning. Each day they went farther south and then farther west. They gradually left the crowded cities, and entered the broad expanses where during the summer the wheat swayed in the breeze and the corn grew tall and strong. Still farther, they began to see cattle grazing on lands where nothing else seemed to grow except scraggly grass and a few bushes. They passed feeding lots where thousands of cattle were corralled behind fences to be fattened for slaughter. It was a sight Eve had never seen before. The steaks they ate in this beef-growing country were fit for a king, and large enough for cowboys to consume, not intended for a city appetite like Eve's.

Far on the horizon, mountains began to appear. The road stretched like a ribbon into the far beyond. They could see miles and miles in all directions, with nothing to obstruct their view. The air smelled fresh and it seemed like ages since they had left the snow country of the north. But it was not summer yet here either, as Ed and Eve discovered when they stopped at a roadside recreation area to stretch their legs and rest a while before continuing on again. The brisk wind almost toppled them over as they got out of the car. Only with the greatest difficulty were they able to set their thermos bottles on the picnic table and they had to hold on to their cups and sandwiches to keep them from blowing away. The winds became even gustier and road signs began to appear, warning travelers of dangerous cross currents.

"If the winds can be this strong on a sunny day like today, I wonder how they are in a real storm?" Eve wondered. "I suppose that since the Texans boast of everything in their state as being bigger and greater, it's only natural that even their winds would be fiercer than elsewhere."

The road eventually took them higher and closer to the mountains. The mountain sides were covered with pine trees, with snow on their tops. The scenery became more and more rugged, with craggy rocks jutting out on the roadsides. The air felt much colder. The wind was piercingly cold and seemed to blow into their motel room under the door. On the fourth day of their trip, they reached the highest point in the mountains and then began to descend to lower altitudes as they turned south. It began to get warmer. They took off their sweaters and eventually turned on the air conditioner. Another half day and they finally reached their destination at a resort in the desert area.

"You made a good choice, darling," Eve said as she looked around. The resort was made up of individual small cabins surrounding a central green area with grass, cacti and trees, some of which were palms. A gardener was watering and his efforts certainly bore fruit in the luscious green of the grass and trees. A swimming pool was the focal point around which the day's activities seemed to occur, judging from the swimmers splashing in it.

Eve and Ed soon got settled and spent their days swimming in the pool and sunning themselves. Some days they took time off to visit the local shops to purchase curios for themselves and gifts for family. Each evening they went to a different restaurant, seeking out colorful places where gourmet foods were served. One day they met a vacationing couple, Bill and Beth Perkins from their home state, and from then on the four of them spent much time together, exploring the surrounding areas and making the side trips Ed had planned back home. As they were returning from one of these outings they saw a billboard advertising the best steaks ever at a restaurant in the little town they were passing through.

"Let's go in and have our dinner here," suggested Beth. The foursome went in and gave their order. They waited eagerly for the steaks. Hiking in the fresh air searching for natural sculptures in the area had made them very hungry. The steaks were brought to the table, and at first glance they did indeed look good. Eve tasted hers. She glanced at the others and asked, "Are your steaks hot? Mine seems to be all cold in the center."

Ed replied, "So is mine." Beth and Bill concurred.

Just then the waitress came around to inquire, "Is everything O.K.?"

"The steaks are cold," Eve replied. "You advertised such good steaks but these are far from good."

41

"Oh, I'm sorry. I'll take them back to the kitchen to be warmed up," the waitress apologized as she picked up the plates. They sat talking while they waited for the plates to reappear. They wondered why it was taking so long. After quite some time the waitress returned, placing new plates with large sizzling hot steaks before them. All this time Ed had been glancing toward the kitchen with a strange look on his face. "I knew we'd get new steaks," he finally volunteered.

"How did you know?" asked Eve.

"Well, something happened earlier that made me certain that the cook wouldn't just warm up the meat for us," he replied.

"What do you mean? Don't keep us in suspense," Bill prodded.

"After we had given our order to the waitress, I went down to the men's room to wash up. While I was washing my hands, I saw a soiled apron hanging on a hook. A man came out of the toilet stall, put on the apron and then went to the other faucet and rinsed his hands. I asked him if he was the chef and he said he was. I told him I was a physician and a health department official, and I asked him if that was the way he had been taught to wash his hands. As a food handler, didn't he know any better? I told him he should wash his hands using soap to work up a good lather. I then proceeded to demonstrate proper handwashing techniques."

"Wow! Didn't he get mad?" Eve asked.

"I guess so. He looked angry and annoyed and didn't say anything right away. But after a while he said I was absolutely right and went back to the faucet and began washing his hands the way I had showed him. He pointed to a sign on the wall which said that at this restaurant they washed their hands after toilet."

"Good for you!" exclaimed Bill.

Ed continued, "After the waitress returned our plates to the kitchen, I saw the chef peering through the glass on the door. He must have gotten a jolt when he saw that they were from our table. I was absolutely certain then that he would do the best he could for us, and consequently we were served these quality steaks. He couldn't take a chance of having the license for the restaurant revoked by the health department."

Bill and Beth gazed at Ed in wonder and Eve said, "You really had the courage. But I guess I probably would have done the same."

Ed went on, "You know the rules of sanitation are so deeply ingrained in me that regardless of where I am, I still feel it my obligation to try to correct things if I see something wrong."

"It's the same with me," Eve said. "I was once in a cafeteria where one of the women dishing out the food behind the counter was coughing her head off. I asked for the manager. I left my place in the cafeteria line and marched straight to her and told her what was happening. She thanked me for alerting her."

"I guess we'll call you two Mr. and Mrs. Health Officers next time we go out to eat, so the waitress will hear and we'll get the best they have," said Bill with a hearty laugh. As they were ready to leave Ed told the waitress, "Congratulate the chef on our behalf for the good food."

It was already dark. Eve laid her head on Ed's shoulder as they sat alone in the back seat. He took her hand and pressed it. There was silence as they sped on in the dark. Bill suggested taking a short detour before returning to the resort. He drove to the top of a small mountain to view the lights of the city below. They quietly watched the dazzling sight of thousands of lights flickering in the darkness below.

One day Ed suggested to Eve that the two of them make a trip to a small town up in the mountains that he had read had an excellent climate, clean air and many recreational opportunities. It was an easy two-hour drive from their resort. The air was much cooler than in the desert, but the sun was shining from a clear blue sky and it felt very springlike even though it was only February.

"I could stand this climate very well," Ed said. The town was very picturesque and reminded them remotely of some of the mountain villages they had seen in the Swiss Alps. It was surrounded by forests with tall pines which, according to the brochures, were used by people from the desert in the summer to escape the dreadful heat. As they stopped for a traffic light, an elderly woman stepped up to the open car window and said that their car license indicated they were from her home state. The traffic light changed several times before they finished talking to the woman. They learned each other's names and made plans to be driven around the city and its surroundings by the woman and her husband, later that day.

The older couple picked them up at the designated place. They were enthusiastic about the town and everything it had to offer. They showed Eve and Ed the county hospital, the veteran's hospital, the two colleges and some of the residential areas. It seemed too good to be true. The town offered so much and the people seemed so friendly.

On their way back, Ed said, "I guess we've found the place where we can retire. It has the four seasons but nothing like the freezing winters we have up north, nor the hot humid summers. Did you notice how easy it was to breathe there? And all that sunshine! This booklet says the sun shines almost every day, even during the rainy season when it rains only part of the day. We wouldn't feel isolated. It seems to have culture and everything we need, and it isn't too far from the lower deserts either, and its big cities."

Eve agreed, but did not quite share his enthusiasm. She was already thinking of her job back home and feeling some longing for it. "Let's not be too hasty in making a decision," she said.

"We'll study up on every aspect of the place, its taxes, real estate values, industries etc.," Ed replied.

"You're very good at that. I know you look into things thoroughly before you decide on anything," Eve said.

"You don't sound too enthusiastic."

"Well, I don't think we're ready yet, but it won't hurt us to get to know more of the place."

"We'll be ready before you know it," was Ed's reply, which Eve did not dispute.

The three weeks they had for their vacation went all too quickly and in no time at all it seemed, they were on their way home again. They again encountered icy roads and drove through snow-storms with warnings to travelers over the radio. One day they had to stop at a motel in mid-afternoon because it was too dangerous to drive further. The farther east they drove the more congested the traffic became.

"Is this what you like?" Ed asked sarcastically. "Where is the relaxed state of mind you achieved during our vacation?

You already look all keyed up, keeping up with this traffic."

"What's wrong with being alert? You can't drive anywhere if you don't keep your wits about you," she replied defensively.

They reached their home-town at the rush hour, when the roads were jammed. The cars whizzed by, and the noise and smells were overwhelming. Even Eve was not overly enthusiastic about being back in the rush of things quite so suddenly.

"It would be nice to slow down just a little and to live a more leisurely life," she thought. Instead she had to get herself back in a frame of mind to return to the office by the next morning. The evening was a busy one of unpacking, sorting out dirty clothes and putting away the summer clothes to await the warmer days of next summer. They were so busy and so exhausted that they had no inclination to continue the argument that had started before they reached home. They finally went to sleep, to await the ring of the alarm clock early the next morning.

CHAPTER FIVE

Eve was welcomed back with cheery greetings. No major problems had occurred during her absence. She joked, "I should go away oftener. Then things would go smoother here at the office."

"No, that's not the point at all, it's just that we save everything for your return," one of the staff replied.

"Well, don't spoil my first day back by dumping them all in my lap at once," Eve countered.

"No, we'll give them to you one at a time as soon as you get settled."

"You look real relaxed and tanned," another complimented.

"I worked hard at it. I wondered when one of you was going to say something about my tan," Eve teased.

It felt good to be back. Bertha brought in the mail that had accumulated during Eve's absence. It would take a full week or more before all the mail was dealt with. Bertha also told Eve about her appointments. It looked like a busy time ahead, but Eve thrived on it. However, she could not long bask in the relaxed state she had acquired on her vacation. She needed to be on her toes to make wise decisions and have her best wits about her. When she looked at herself in the mirror at noon she saw she had already lost her placid look. She did not feel tense however, and seemed still somewhat detached from things. Before long though she would become enmeshed in them again, and they would be very much a part of her. It was a strange feeling to be able to handle problems in this detached and objective manner, almost as though she didn't really care. It would make everything much easier to handle and not take so much out of her, if she could keep her inner self apart from her job.

She remembered how she had agonized when she had still been attending seriously ill patients. She worried along with the family as she watched their progress. Often she could not sleep at night when she had an especially sick patient. She felt a great sense of loss and fretted that she had failed to do her best if the patient died. On the other hand, she rejoiced greatly and thanked God if the patient recovered.

Since Eve became so thoroughly involved with her entire being and emotions in anything she undertook, it had been wonderful to have Ed's shoulder to lean on. He calmed her when the disappointments came. At other times the triumphs seemed greater and the joy more profound when she shared them with him. Because Eve was a rather emotional person and felt frustrations, worries and failures deeply, she needed Ed very much. By sharing these with him, she was able to gain strength from him and shed her own feelings of inadequacy more easily. She readily acknowledged that her greatest growth as a career woman had occurred after her marriage. During their years together, she had often asked for Ed's opinion when she had to make an important decision. Although she did not always follow his suggestions, it helped her weigh the relative merits of the various alternatives and the final outcome was probably the sounder for it. Eve was certain that for her to be a successful woman and to gain complete self-fulfillment as a person, she was in need of both her career and her marriage. Ed was certainly the man behind the woman. She hoped she had also been the woman behind the man for him.

It was probably not always easy for Ed to have such an independent career woman as his wife. Home and hearth, of necessity, played a secondary role in Eve's life, as had occurred when the German measles clinics took her entire time and attention. Eve felt Ed's distress very acutely now that he was semiretired. She realized that his feelings of resentment toward her still working were not due to envy or jealousy, but plainly to loneliness. How she wished she could accommodate his wishes and retire. But no, for her that was impossible.

Eve pulled herself back to the task at hand. She had to prepare herself for the many conferences and meetings that were scheduled. Tomorrow she had an important meeting with her key staff, to prepare for the budget for the following fiscal year. It would be necessary to deny many requests for new funds. Procedures that were not productive or were wasteful would need to be revised. Eve encouraged innovative changes and experimentation at all times, but if they proved unsuccessful it was necessary to drop them and try something better. One troublesome area had been the waiting periods patients had to experience while attending clinics. A project was underway to see how this time could be used to best advantage by providing learning experiences for patients the health field, through group discussions, movies and making appropriate literature available for patients to read. None of them had proved to be especially fruitful thus far.

Another area of priority was to prepare several nurses to take over some of the responsibilities that were generally considered to be those of the physician, because of the increasing patient load and the difficulty in recruiting more physicians to the agency. Such a training program would initially decrease the efficiency of services to patients, and would be quite expensive and time-consuming, but in the long run the agency would benefit. Each consultant in Eve's department was a specialist, and included such disciplines as social workers, home economists, nutritionists, and health educators, in addition to the physicians, dentists, and nurses. It was Eve's job to coordinate the various activities, to iron out professional differences and to make decisions when the staff had arrived at an impasse. She usually delegated to smaller groups the responsibility of working out the details of new plans and to bring the draft to her for final approval or to be discussed together with a larger group before being implemented. She was mulling over the recent suggestions from her staff when Bertha came to tell her that a few of the staff wanted an early appointment to discuss ways in which they would bé better informed of decisions made by their superiors and the reasons for them. Eve set a time and went back to her program planning. At the end of the day she put away the many sheets spread on her desk to be taken out again tomorrow. She was surprised to see that everyone else had already left. She closed the door of her office, tired, but glad to be back, and satisfied with her day.

When she arrived home Ed did not meet her at the door with his usual cheery greeting. Then she heard some rustling upstairs and ran up. She found him reading a book. "I guess you didn't hear me come in, but here I am," Eve said.

"Oh, I heard you drive in," he said and continued to read.

"I see," replied Eve, and went into the bedroom to change

from her office clothes into something more comfortable. She then went downstairs to prepare supper without saying anything more to Ed.

He followed her soon after, and began to set the table. "I hope things went well at the office," he said.

"Oh, so-so," replied Eve, without elaborating. She thought, "I can play the game of silence as well as you, if that's the way you want it."

They ate their supper with a minimum of conversation. The air was definitely chilly between them, but neither referred to it. After clearing the table and stacking the dishes in the dishwasher, they went back upstairs, Eve to read the newspaper that had just arrived and Ed his book. There was a loud silence. Eve tried to read but it was difficult for her to concentrate. She was too aware of Ed's presence, but he seemed oblivious of hers. She threw the paper aside and went to the bedroom, closing the door behind her with a bang. She was finding it difficult to control herself. Her anger was rising by the minute.

"Here I come home from a busy day at work, hoping to be able to relax and enjoy the evening with Ed and maybe reminisce about our trip, but instead I get the silent treatment," she fumed. Finally she stalked back into the room where Ed was and threw at him, "What's the idea? What have I done to deserve this kind of treatment from you?"

"You don't know?"

"I certainly do not," she yelled.

"There's no point in talking to you when you're in that mood," he declared self-righteously.

"Me in a mood! What about you? I come home expecting to spend a nice evening with you. But nothing of the sort. You hardly know I exist?"

"I'll talk to you later when you've quieted down and can listen," and with that Ed left the room.

Eve was ready to hit him. Instead she took up the paper again and pretended to read. "I'll be darned if I make the first move." She was seething with fury. Once or twice she was about to get up to go to Ed but then she sat down again. The minutes ticked by with no move on the part of either of them. Finally after what seemed like an hour though in reality it was no more than about fifteen minutes, Ed returned and asked, "Are you ready to talk now?"

Eve did not reply.

"I was worrying about you for about an hour before you came home."

"Why should you do that?" Eve asked in amazement.

"Maybe you didn't look at your watch, but do you know you were an hour late getting home tonight?"

Eve was rankled. "I didn't know you kept that close tabs on me. What did you think I was doing? I was at the office with my desk piled high, and it took me a while. I couldn't just leave everything."

"Here we go again. Can't you talk in a reasonable manner? Didn't you ever think of me here at home, waiting and waiting? You could at least have telephoned and told me you would be late."

"I didn't think I had to report every minute of my time. I'm a grown-up person you know, yet you treat me like a child."

"You try sitting here by yourself and you'll see what it's like," retorted Ed.

"I guess it would be better that I live my own life and you live yours. I can't be bossed like this! Find someone else, I'm going my own way," Eve cried and she left the room. "I'm going to bed now."

She curled herself up tightly on her own side of the bed, seething with fury.

"I'll move tomorrow. How can I carry on my job with this kind of pettiness facing me at home every night? I hate him, I hate him. I won't be able to sleep all night, how will I face tomorrow at the office all upset?"

Ed was quiet on his side of the bed. Eve had no idea of what he was thinking. Finally she quieted down a bit, and began to cry. "He's just not fair, all he thinks of is himself. Why doesn't he get himself something to do? He shouldn't be so tied to me that it feels like a yoke around my neck."

After some considerable time Ed turned around and at the same time Eve turned around too and somehow found herself in his arms. "I'm sorry, I just didn't look at the clock. I didn't realize it was that late when I left the office," she sobbed.

"I'm sorry, too. I should have been more understanding. But you must understand it's an awfully long day here alone," Ed said.

"Why don't you do something so the time won't be so long?" Eve asked.

"There isn't much to do in the wintertime. I can't work in the garden. I can read only so much, and write letters. The chores around the house are soon done and I can't go anywhere without you." Eve quieted down and thought of an acquaintance of theirs who was also retired and was making a pest of himself. His wife was still working, and he had gotten into the habit of coming downtown each noon to eat. He latched on to any acquaintance he knew, without taking into consideration whether he was welcome or not. A time or two he had joined Eve at her table. It annoyed her because she certainly did not want to eat her meals with him. She began to avoid that restaurant, or if she did go there she looked around first and if she saw him, would seat herself at the opposite end of the room.

She certainly did not want Ed to become such a parasite. "Oh, dear, I'm no good for him anymore and he certainly isn't helping me. It probably would be best after all if we separated. Then he could find someone compatible to share his life with." She kept these thoughts to herself. She didn't want to start another quarrel, but it was a long time before either of them fell asleep. Although they had each said they were sorry, they had not really forgiven each other for the slights each thought the other had committed.

Eve somehow got through the next day but she was very depressed. She called Ed at noon just to let him know she was thinking of him. That evening Ed was very solicitous of her, and on the surface everything was very peaceful, but the gap between them widened.

CHAPTER SIX

Eve began to sleep poorly. Either the night was far spent before she fell asleep, or if she did fall asleep quickly, she would wake up later and stay awake until the wee hours of the morning. One evening in exasperation Ed told her, "Take a sleeping pill."

"I will not. If I can't fall asleep naturally I'm not going to get myself dependent on drugs. Do you want me to become a drug addict?"

As a result of her sleeplessness Eve was very tired during the day. She also became very tense and her appetite fell off. She had difficulty keeping her temper and used all her strength to discipline herself so her feelings would not show, and to appear unruffled whatever the situation. She had a role to play now that did not allow her to show her emotions. She felt worse when she was bogged down with routine matters, day after day. At such times she felt ready to comply with Ed's wishes and give up her job. But her spirits soared at least temporarily when she was faced with the challenges of new developments and new programs. Her enthusiasm was kindled anew, her eyes sparkled again and she felt new energy flow through her. This had always been the wonderful part of her job — just as things seemed to settle down into a rut and she began to feel bored, something new would develop. There were still so many unexplored horizons where she could wander and work on new projects.

As the weeks went by, and Eve became ever more involved in her new plans, she was able to forget her fatigue while at work and somehow found the strength to function at near her usual capacity. She looked forward to each day at work, while at the same time she dreaded going home. She couldn't bear to look at Ed's downcast and unhappy face. She herself began to lose weight and developed dark rings around her eyes. She was pushing herself beyond her strength, riding on the crest of nervous energy. It seemed ever more important that she have the opportunity to see her efforts to fruition. She knew she wouldn't be around long enough to see the end results of the programs, but she wanted to get them well on the way at least.

Ed feared she might have a nervous breakdown with her non-stop activity, so one day he suggested, "Let's go for a weekend to the retreat center. I know we decided earlier not to go, but you're so keyed up, a couple of days in the country will do you good. I'm sure we can still get reservations. It might give us a chance to see where we're at. We can't continue this kind of a life."

"I guess you're right," Eve admitted.

Right after work on a Friday afternoon, they drove off to the retreat center to spend the weekend. They knew some of the other people going. The streets were choked with cars all with seemingly the same destination, away from downtown. It seemed they could never get out. It would have been faster to walk. Eve's frayed nerves were almost at the breaking point, but eventually they were able to leave the traffic jam behind, and speed to their destination some fifty miles away. They had never been to the lodge, but the directions seemed clear enough. They were to turn off the highway into a wooded area a mile from the outskirts of a small town they went through.

"This must be it," said Ed. They turned off. It wasn't a very good road. The early spring rains mixed with sleet had made it very soft. The ruts got deeper and deeper as they drove along, until their car suddenly got stuck in deep mud.

"What are we going to do now?" wailed Eve.

Ed got out of the car and jumped across a ditch onto a field that had a stubble of short stalks after the cutting of last year's harvest. The ground here was higher and drier than the road. He looked around and saw a farmhouse not far away at the end of the road. "Let's walk up to the house and see if we can get some help," he called out to Eve.

A man and three children were in the yard. They stared as Eve and Ed approached them. Ed inquired if they could help him get the car out of the mud. The man and the oldest boy, both wearing patched-up jeans and slouchy old hats, agreed to pull the car out with their horse. They walked back to the car, the man leading a large farm horse. They harnessed the horse to the rear bumper of the car to pull it out backward onto firmer ground. Squelch, first one wheel, then another and finally the whole car was back on solid ground, mud dripping from all four wheels. The farmer refused the payment Ed offered him. To him it was just a good neighborly deed. Eve and Ed were profuse in their thank-yous. Before they left, they received detailed instructions on how to get to the lodge. They reached the highway and drove slowly back, passing two side roads before they saw the one they should have taken. This one had crushed gravel on it and a sign with an arrow and the name of the lodge posted at the turn-off, which they had missed earlier. After parking their car they walked toward the lodge. The beauty of it and its surroundings impressed them greatly. It was early spring, the air was still cool but there was a mildness to it that promised warmer days to come. Snow was heaped under the great pines but on the sunny slopes there were some patches of dark earth. There was a faint greenish tint in the leaf trees as though they were showing off the life in them.

The lodge was built of brown logs as was the two-story guest house with its rows of private rooms on either side of a long corridor. Eve and Ed were assigned a corner room on the second floor. It contained two single beds with natural stained wooden head- and foot-boards, a matching chest of drawers, a desk, and two chairs with wicker seats. A little alcove served as the clothes closet with hangers on nails in the walls. Matching cotton bedspreads and drapes had a rustic pattern of greens, browns, yellows and oranges.

The view from the two windows was breathtaking. Giant Norway pines swayed gently in the breeze. At the bottom of a steep slope they could see a lake covered with ice. There was a boat house near the lake. "I can just imagine how lovely it is here in the summertime, with swimming off that beach and boats out on the lake," said Eve. They quickly changed into slacks, pullover sweaters and comfortable shoes, and walked over to the lodge which housed the dining room, library, meeting rooms and a small chapel. Others already ahead of them were in the dining room, standing at the large windows which surrounded the room on all sides, admiring the beautiful view. The sun was just beginning to dip behind the horizon of trees casting long dark shadows.

A tantalizing smell of food came from the kitchen. Barry Jones, who was in charge of the retreat, clapped his hands urging everybody to take a seat at one of the four round tables. He asked Ed to give the blessing. Ed thanked God for the safe trip to this beautiful spot in nature, and prayed that the weekend would be beneficial and that everyone would return home with renewed spirits. He asked for the food to be blessed for the strengthening of bodies.

Some of the members had been recruited to carry in the food for this first meal, with the task to be rotated before each succeeding meal. They brought in huge platters of country-fried, golden chicken with mounds of mashed potatoes, carrots, jello salad. There was homemade bread, milk in pitchers, coffee and a peach cobbler for dessert. The platters and dishes held enough food for two and even three extra helpings. One of the men told Eve, "You better eat enough now, you look half starved." Not surprisingly she had a good appetite. It had been several weeks since she had been able to eat without forcing herself. There were oh's and ah's to be heard and with some imagination one could almost hear the people purr with contentment as they ate. Finally, when they could eat no more, the men and women pushed themselves away from the tables. Everyone carried a load of dishes into the kitchen, stacking them in the assigned places for the kitchen help to tackle them. The group then gathered in the library to learn about the schedule of events for the next two days and to participate in the opening event which would set the tone for the retreat.

The participants were all married couples. They represented various churches and denominations. Eve and Ed knew a few of them, and one couple belonged to the same club they did. The club was social in character and met once a month in members' homes and for special events such as dinners, theater and the like. Eve and Ed had joined the club to make up for their lack of a social life outside of their professions.

Barry Jones, who was there without his wife, was a lay leader in his church and was experienced as a group discussion leader. The topic for the retreat was self-fulfillment with discussions for self-improvement. After explaining the practical details of the schedule, Barry asked them to clasp hands as he read the Bible chapter on love, from the letter to the Corinthians. Eve was ready to cry when she listened to the familiar words. She felt a great sense of loss and loneliness, a nostalgia for days that seemed ever gone. They had had a full day and felt very tired, so she and Ed decided to turn in after a short walk around the lodge. They saw other couples sauntering along in the dark also. Eve expected another sleepless night, but to her pleasant surprise, when she woke up it was time for breakfast. They joined the others in the dining room. The kitchen detail brought in stacks of pancakes with lots of butter and syrup. The aroma of freshly brewed coffee filled the room, perking up Eve's senses even before she tasted it.

Soon after breakfast the group gathered in the library. Barry started the discussion by stating how his religion was able to bring him fulfillment. He drew others into the conversation, urging them to express themselves. As is usual with group discussions, the beginning was slow, but eventually it warmed up. There was no great controversy among the group as far as the religious aspects were concerned. Gradually the talk led to how the various persons perceived their own self-fulfillment in the here and now. Both Eve and Ed had been quiet up till now. But now Eve felt an urge to talk and said, "I am not satisfied in getting my own self-fulfillment through the accomplishments of my husband as so many women do, although I rejoice in them. I feel I must get my own ego satisfaction through myself and what I do. I feel each person, whether man or woman, should develop to the utmost his God-given talents and gain gratification through them. At the same time, because of personal self-fulfillment, he or she should be able to live in a mature, sharing experience with the spouse, on an equal footing: I feel that the wife should give moral and emotional support to the husband in his endeavors, but likewise, the husband should support the wife in hers. If the woman wants to stay at home, that's her privilege, but for those who do not find satisfaction in the home alone, they should be allowed to pursue their talents outside of the home. She shouldn't have to stay at home just because she is a woman."

This opened up a Pandora's box. There were a few women, along with many of the men, who agreed with Eve. But it was surprising to Eve that the women themselves were largely opposed to gaining fulfillment through accomplishments outside the home. One woman who was a teacher said, "I wouldn't work another day if it wasn't necessary financially. I'd much rather stay at home." Eve wondered about this because this woman talked with great enthusiasm about incidents in her classroom to anyone she could corner.

Another woman vehemently defended her position. She seemed very angry when she retorted to Eve, "I have no desire for self glory. I get complete satisfaction through my husband and his career. I think it's a woman's responsibility to stay at home and work there for her husband and children, and see that they're comfortable, well fed and clothed." Eve must have touched a raw nerve. She knew that this woman was very capable, was active as a Sunday School teacher and participated in community and political activities. It was also true that her husband had an important position and was an accomplished public speaker.

Eve replied, "I don't mean that we should all work for pay. You are certainly making your contribution through all your volunteer activities. But I still feel that when a woman gains recognition for herself, she is a better mate and companion to her husband. Besides, I would feel guilty if I did not use the education my father provided for me, at great sacrifice to himself, or if I were not doing the work wherein I find fulfillment. Part of my satisfaction comes from being able to help others. Doesn't the Bible admonish us not to hide our talents under a bushel? I don't think it was said just to men."

Ed interjected, "I fully agree with Eve's need to work. We both have enjoyed a well-rounded life and have had so much to share. In supporting Eve in leading an independent professional life, I think it contributed greatly to the success of our marriage."

Someone asked, "Wouldn't a conflict arise if either the working wife or husband was to be transferred elsewhere?"

A woman spoke up, "Of course the wife would transfer with her husband."

"What if the wife was to be transferred?"

Eve replied, "Why shouldn't the husband follow his wife, if her career depended on it?"

"What about *his* career?"

"Maybe they would have to commute to each other. It has happened."

"It certainly wouldn't work well with young children in the home," one woman commented.

"I agree there would be a conflict, even without children. The couple would have to determine whose career at that point was more important, the husband's or the wife's," Eve admitted, thinking of her own situation with Ed. With indignation she told herself, "Why of course my career is more important now. Ed doesn't even have a career anymore. Why should I sacrifice myself?" She sat back and listened as some of the other women spoke up. One admitted that at this stage in life she was completely contented to stay at home and have her husband work. She liked the security her husband provided her. She did no volunteer work, but rather filled in the afternoon hours by playing golf or bridge with some other women. "It would be hard for me to get out of the comfortable rut I'm in."

Another woman said, "I'm not trained for any job, but a few times a week I go to an old people's home and visit with the folks there, reading to them or writing letters for them."

One of the husbands spoke up. "My wife used to work as a nurse, but as I got ahead in my profession, I wanted her to quit, because I didn't want it to look as though we needed the money."

"Shame on you," Eve called out.

"Well, she's doing volunteer work now and that's important too," was the reply.

Another woman replied, "But I love doing nursing and since there is a shortage of nurses I feel that my services are needed. We don't need the extra money, but my work is so important. I don't care what it looks to the world and Bob agrees with me." Bob nodded his agreement.

The talk was so lively that Barry Jones just sat back. Eve wasn't sure if he was completely happy with the turn of the discussion, away from the religious aspects and into this controversy about women's rights. Now the men took over. "I wish my wife could get out of the house more. It seems we don't have too many things to talk about, when I'm in the outside world and she's always home. I have more fun with the boys. I love my wife, but it seems we have grown apart to some extent."

"You're always out with the boys leaving me home alone," the wife remarked bitterly.

Another man said, "My wife is very intelligent, and although she doesn't work outside the home, she is a great help to me. When I have a difficult decision to make or a problem to tackle, I duscuss it with her and she helps me come to a solution."

"I'll bet she doesn't get paid for helping you. And I'm sure you get all the credit for it. Why shouldn't your employer know that your wife helps you?" asked Eve.

"That's a novel thought. But I'm not so sure my employer would approve of my talking of my business matters with my wife," was the reply.

They broke up for lunch. Eve felt some hostility in the air. Those who disagreed with her kept out of her way, but the few women who sided with her came up to her to tell her so. Eve was sure that no minds were changed, but at least everyone knew where the others stood, and if some understanding grew out of the discussions, something had been gained.

The weekend went very fast. The men and women were riding on a crest of exhilaration and excitement, intermingled with anger as they defended their own views.

During one of the breaks, Eve felt she had to go alone on a quiet walk to still her turbulent thoughts. The time was fast approaching when she and Ed would have to meet their own personal problem head on. She watched a squirrel scamper among the snow and dried leaves under the trees and disappear. There were other animal tracks in the snow but Ed was not with her to help identify them.

As she walked along deep in thought, she met Barry Jones. He stopped and said, "What you said in these meetings upsets me very much. Up to now I couldn't imagine my wife working outside the home. But now that all our children are in school, she has become very restless. I wonder if I have the right to insist that she continue to stay at home. I think she would like to get herself a job. I'll have to think about it some more."

The last event of the retreat was an informal worship service in the chapel. The group solemnly gathered as one of the members quietly played the organ. It was dim, with only the light of the candles flickering on the altar.

A few weeks later Eve was sitting in a crowded auditorium waiting for a meeting to start, when she felt a tap on her shoulder and turned around to see who it was. It was Barry Jones. After exchanging a few words of greeting he said, "May I sit here next to you? I just have to tell you what happened at our house after the retreat. I swallowed my pride and encouraged my wife to find the job she wanted. The only condition I laid down was that she should be home when the younger children came home from school. She is working now, and is very happy. She is doing a very good job as a free lance saleswoman. Soon she'll earn more than I do, but that doesn't bother me anymore. We're so much happier together now. She used to be so frustrated and took it out on me. It seems that the kids are doing better in school too, when there isn't the constant bickering going on at home. Our mealtimes are really fun now, because my wife seems to have the most interesting experiences of us all and she makes us all laugh at her stories. Thank you so much for opening my eyes."

"Something good came out of the retreat after all. I was afraid that we all came with our own special prejudices and left there with the same ones. Thank you for telling me. I wish you and your wife all the luck in the world," Eve smiled.

CHAPTER SEVEN

It was increasingly difficult for Eve to hide her feelings from Bertha. Bertha would look at Eve when she thought Eve didn't see her doing it. There was a questioning look in her eyes. One day she told Eve, "You look ill. Don't you think you should practice what you preach, and have a medical examination?"

Eve replied, "Oh, there's nothing wrong with me. This is just such a busy time. When things settle down a bit, I won't feel so rushed."

"Well, you look awfully pale and thin to me."

"You need new glasses! Don't you worry about me!"

Bertha asked if Eve would like to have her mid-morning coffee. "Yes, please," Eve replied. Soon Bertha came in with a pot of hot water. Eve measured a heaping spoonful of instant coffee into the cup she kept in her desk drawer, and Bertha poured the water over it.

"You should relax more and take a break like everyone else does," said Bertha. "Why don't you go down to the coffee shop in the basement rather than continuing your work even while you're supposed to refresh yourself with this coffee?"

"Oh, don't be so bossy and stop acting like a mother hen around me," Eve exclaimed.

"Somebody has to look after you. You don't seem to have enough sense to do it yourself," Bertha retorted.

"What a way to talk to your boss!"

It was true that Bertha was a bit bossy. She and Eve had worked together many years. She was somewhat older than Eve and did not mince her words. At first it had annoyed and bothered Eve. Being a young executive, she felt her secretary should show her more respect. But after she herself matured, she did not need to be flattered to the same extent as before by those around her. Bertha had good, common sense, and she told Eve when she thought some of the rules and procedures in the agency were "silly." Occasionally they were modified because of her criticisms.

Eve had come to depend very heavily on Bertha. After so many years together, Bertha pretty well knew what she wanted and seemed able to read her thoughts about many things even before Eve spoke. Sometimes Eve put Bertha on the spot when she wanted something in a hurry. This usually happened when she got a telephone call asking for information. Bertha would have a blank look for a second after such a request, then her eyes would brighten and she would say, "Oh, I know what you want. It's in file number three in the middle drawer. I'll get it in a jiffy," and she would.

Since Bertha could read Eve and her thoughts so well, Eve was apprehensive that she would soon learn about her troubles with Ed, if she hadn't already guessed. Bertha knew that when Ed still worked, he and Eve had always gone off to lunch together if their schedules permitted, and also knew they were a very devoted couple. It must seem odd to Bertha now that Eve so seldom mentioned Ed. On the other hand Eve never shared her personal or social life with Bertha and Ed no longer belonged to her office life. Eve considered her secretary a friend, but in a rather impersonal way, sharing with her only the everyday life of the office. Now she wondered. Was she deluding herself of her capability of keeping her private life secret from Bertha?

In a public office one could expect anything and be prepared to help people with all kinds of problems. So often one heard the complaint that governmental agencies shuttled people from one place to another without helping them, always passing the buck. Eve insisted that if someone called or came in with a problem the agency was unable to deal with, the staff person should call and find out first which office or agency could help before sending the client there. Bertha and her reference file of other agencies and the services they provided were a great help.

Eve remembered a rather scary incident that had occurred the previous summer. It was the noon hour and most employees had gone out to lunch. Bertha was at her desk and Eve was finishing her work so she could get out to lunch too. Just as she was about to leave she saw an old man in worn-out clothing approaching Bertha's desk with a shuffling gait. He was carrying a cloth sack that looked like a laundry bag over his shoulder. Eve heard him say to Bertha, "I wanna see a doctor."

"What is your trouble?"

"I got sores all over my legs," and with that the man proceeded to pull up his trouser legs, "Do you want to see them?" Bertha later told Eve that his legs were full of festering boils with the pus running down his legs. She told the man, "Oh my, they do look bad. You need treatment right away. You'll have to go to the emergency room at the general hospital. I'll show you how to get there."

The man replied, "No, I ain't going to no general hospital. Can't your doctors do something?"

"I'm afraid we can't help you here. We're not equipped to do this kind of work here," Bertha told him. "The general hospital emergency room is supposed to take care of everybody in the county. Where do you live?"

"Under the bridge."

"Under the bridge?" was Bertha's astonished reply. "How long have you been there?"

"Two weeks."

"Where did you live before that?"

"At L————Penitentiary."

"Oh! Why were you there?"

"For murder."

"You were? Whom did you kill?"

"A guy."

"Aren't you sorry now you did it?"

"No, he had it coming."

With that Bertha came into Eve's office. "You heard what's going on out there. What shall I do?" Eve came out and talked to the man. She found out that he had indeed been released from prison a couple of weeks earlier out-of-state, had run out of funds and had no job nor resources. His entire worldly possessions were in the sack he was carrying.

"Will you give me permission to see what we can do for you not only for your medical problem, but also for your other problems?" she asked the man.

"It's O.K. with me."

Eve went back to her office and wondered where she could ask for help. She had never been confronted with a problem like this. She thought, "Surely the welfare department should know what is available for released prisoners." She called and the welfare director was in and answered the telephone. Eve told him her strange tale. She was advised that there was a special office in the city that provided help to released prisoners, and that they could help the man with his medical problem as well as other problems.

Eve telephoned this office and repeated the story to them. They told her to send the man to them. She went out to the man and told him what she had learned. He seemed happy that he would get some help. She had Bertha arrange for transportation for the man to get to the place and soon he was on his way there. After he left Bertha and Eve discussed the sad case. "How could you ask him if he was sorry for having murdered someone? He could have been very angry with you," Eve said.

"I wasn't afraid of him. He seemed pretty washed out. He didn't look as though he could harm anyone."

"I don't suppose he's eaten for days. No wonder he didn't want to walk over to the general hospital. He was probably pretty worn out," Eve said.

"How old do you think he was?" asked Bertha.

"Oh, I suppose in his sixties," Eve guessed.

"That's what I thought at first. His hair was all grey and his face was grey too and wrinkled. So I asked him how old he was and he said he was forty-five," Bertha replied.

"He looked twenty years older. I guess that's what prison does to a person. It's pretty awful, isn't it?"

"What a wasted life," Bertha sighed.

Eve was glad that Bertha was sensitive to the needs of other people. This made her sensitive also to the burdens of her boss. She made them lighter through such simple things as bringing in a cup of coffee and showing that she cared. Yes, Eve was grateful for the contributions of her secretary, even though she had a tendency to be somewhat bossy and over-bearing at times. Eve also admired a former secretary who had retired, who in spite of a serious physical handicap had not given in to her disability, but had overcome it with sheer force of will and carried out all aspects of her job as though there were no handicap. Being surrounded by problems, Eve felt she would be a coward if she left everything now. There were so many people who needed help and could be helped. As long as Eve could help, she felt she should do so. This was where life was being lived, not somewhere in a remote corner of the earth. But Ed's sad face kept creeping into her mind, however much she tried to shut it out. "What am I going to do?" she moaned to herself.

CHAPTER EIGHT

Eve was in the midst of one of her sleepless nights again. She tossed and turned as she tried unsuccessfully to find a comfortable position. She sat up awhile, and stretched her arms, careful not to wake Ed. It was no use. Sleep just would not come. She got up quietly, put on her robe and slippers and walked out of the bedroom, closing the door behind her silently. She walked down the stairs hoping he would not hear the creaking of the steps. She went into the sunroom behind the living room and curled up in the corner chair in front of the windows. Eve closed her eyes and prayed for inner peace. She had to come to some decision. She tried to picture what her life would be like in retirement. She knew she could never make this choice without great qualms, but perhaps she would get over it eventually, and began to list in her mind the pros and cons of retirement.

One of the most important advantages of retirement would be the opportunity to spend all her time with Ed and do those pleasurable things they had never had time for. These included the opportunity to travel, and they both enjoyed traveling greatly. They had visited some of the provinces of Canada, which was Ed's native country and they had been several times to Europe. They had also gone on a Caribbean cruise once, but there were still many places to see. Since their time had always been so limited it seemed they had never had time to really get to know the various places and their peoples, so there were many places they would like to revisit.

Having been so busy in their professional lives, their entire time seemed to be taken up by their jobs, leaving little if any time to cultivate real close friendships. It would be nice to have some close friends to visit and to cultivate them for what they were and not for what they did. It would be nice to be a little frivolous at times.

Eve hated those early morning risings to get to work on time. In the winter it was dark when she had to get up and even in the summer, during daylight time, it seemed as though they got up with the birds. What luxury it would be to be able to sleep as long as you wished and to awaken to your own desire, and not because the alarm clock tells you to. Eve usually gobbled down her breakfast so as not to waste any time. Besides she was still half asleep and couldn't carry on a sensible conversation even if she tried. It was not until after her second cup of coffee that she became alert enough again to be completely aware of her surroundings. A leisurely breakfast would be heavenly. She tried to think of other nice things in retirement. "I suppose I'm too tense. I could enjoy things more if I could relax and take things in stride. I get uptight if things don't go as smoothly as I would like. I'm much too compulsive. I don't know if leisure would correct that or if that's my make-up that I have to live with. But if I weren't compulsive I never would have achieved all I have. Retirement might add years to my life because I suppose I'm burning the candle at both ends, and it must be taking a toll on my life or at least on my health."

Eve's night-time soliloquy continued. "I'm not too fond of these long winters, either. I used to skate when I was younger but after I fell on the ice a few years back I've been afraid of trying again. You can't ski in the city and besides, people don't do cross-country skiing here, they're only interested in downhill skiing and I've never been good at that. I'd like to be in a place where they had little or no winter, but long springtimes and where the summers are not too hot. Here, after the long winter we have a few days of spring and then summer comes with its unbearably hot weather, so you can't sit outdoors much, even in summer, because of the heat in the daytime and the mosquitos in the evening.

"It might be fun and interesting to settle down in a new place. We're kind of in a rut staying here so long. We're both adventurous, having lived in other places during our lifetimes, and courageous enough to try something different again."

She tried hard to think of other advantages. Was retirement a long vacation? Was it leaving all your worries behind and not being responsible for the well-being of others, only for yourself and Ed? Did it give an opportunity to pursue other hobbies besides traveling? "What other hobbies do I have? I guess I could pick up knitting again, I could do more handwork and crafts, or at least develop an interest in them, like other women. I could be more a clinging vine and take pleasure out of leaning more on Ed. I could try taking up afternoon coffee klatches with other women or play bridge — I'd have to learn how first."

"No, no, no. Now I'm getting ridiculous. I could never fill in all my time traveling, or in crafts, dabbling in painting or the like. I don't have any talent for the arts. I can't spent the rest of my life frantically searching for a good time." Eve began to sob. "Retired people aren't considered very bright anymore. People look down on them as though they were in their second childhood."

Her pessimistic thoughts went on. "I can't. I might just as well give up and die, before leading a life such as that. I can't leave all my intellectual pursuits behind. I hate housework; is that all I have to look forward to? Will I have only my cooking to be complimented? What achievement does cooking produce anyway? It tastes good while you're eating it, but it only takes about fifteen minutes to devour even the best of meals that probably took an hour or two to prepare, and then who will ever remember what you made, or who cares? Besides, I'm not that keen on cooking, anyway."

Eve became more and more frantic until she herself realized she was fringing on hysteria, but she could not help herself. "I've worked hard all my life, first at my studies, then in establishing myself in my career and then continuously devising new and better ways to improve our services to other people. I can't quit now, when I'm at the peak of my career and of my life's work. I still have many years ahead of me, productive years of achievement. I'm recognized as someone with authority and even prestige. When you retire you're out. No one gives credit to what you have achieved earlier, you're a 'has been,' 'a nobody.' I couldn't take it. I still want to be a part of the professional scene, with its interesting contacts and meeting important people who use their brains. I have to challenge my brains every day, otherwise I'll get dull like retired people do. It just wouldn't be fair to force me to live my life apart from this and pretend to enjoy an endless time of leisure. I've got to serve other people as long as I can. Why should I have to retire early? Ed worked many years after the normal retirement age. It just isn't fair. It won't be easy to adjust to a new place. If our situations were reversed, I bet Ed wouldn't retire to accommodate me," she sobbed, feeling more and more self-pity. An occasional car passed on the river road, throwing its beam of light into the room where Eve sat huddled.

"No! I am not going to retire until I reach my retirement age and have to leave. What would life without Ed be like? He no doubt would leave me for greener pastures. I'll miss him terribly, but my life would be completely worthless and we'd just quarrel constantly anyway, if we stayed together. I got along alone before we were married and I'm sure I'd adjust easier to that than giving everything up." The next moment Eve was overwhelmed with the sorrow she knew she would feel when she was alone.

"There is no other choice. I've had the better of two worlds so long. I knew it couldn't last. But since I can't have both a husband and a career, I have to choose my career. Oh, how am I going to tell Ed, and how will he take it?"

The night was almost over when Eve crept back into bed. She was not sure whether Ed had missed her, he was so quiet on his side of the bed. If she could only get an hour of sleep before she had to get up again. Tomorrow she would have to tell Ed of her decision, but not until she came home from work.

She thought she would never get through the day. The hours dragged and the tears were not far away. One moment she thought her decision was right. The next moment she moaned, "Oh, my God, what am I doing? I can't live alone."

At supper Eve tried to make small talk so as to delay telling Ed. But the supper could be stretched only so far. She spent a longer time clearing the table and filling the dishwasher than usual. Ed got tired of her dawdling and went upstairs to turn on the television. Finally Eve joined him.

"Please turn the set off, I have something to tell you," she said. He did as she requested and sat back to listen. The words tumbled from her mouth: "I've come to a decision. I've thought it through and considered both the advantages and disadvantages of retirement and find that I must continue working if I want to be true to myself. My career must come first. Maybe in a couple of years it will be easier for me to give all this up, but I just can't do it now."

"I see," replied Ed quietly. Eve waited several minutes for him to say more.

"Is that all you have to say?" she asked.

"Your mind is made up. What can I say?"

"You mean it doesn't matter one way or the other to you?"

No answer. "I guess you don't love me and never have," Eve cried out.

"How can you think that?"

"Here I've been agonizing all these weeks and months over something that doesn't mean a thing to you," Eve sobbed.

"Are you crying for yourself or for me?" Ed asked.

"For both. What will you do?"

"I don't know yet. Does it really matter to you?"

It did not occur to her that during all this time she had been thinking only of the effects of retirement on herself. The "we" of marriage had been replaced by "I." She had not paid much attention to the effect her decision would have on Ed. She knew she would be lonely without him, but her reasoning seemed to indicate that Ed did not have much feeling toward her and could well cope without her. Or if he could not, he could easily find a replacement for her. How little she really knew Ed. Or perhaps she purposely had closed her mind to the possible effects on Ed.

"Why don't you say something?" Eve cried out in desperation. "You don't care." Ed walked out of the room, saying, "We'll talk when you calm down and will listen."

"But I *am* listening and waiting to hear your reaction." Eve was ready to throw things around in her frustration at her inability to reach Ed as always happened when they quarreled.

Early in her marriage, Eve found out that her temperament was completely different from Ed's. He never lost his cool. He refused to enter a quarrel, but would walk away from it until the other person cooled down. But this just made Eve angrier, until she was ready to explode. She controlled her feelings quite well at the office and in public, but she felt that at home she should be able to show her true feelings. She wanted to be able to discuss their differences. Ed wanted this too, but in a calm and detached manner. Eve's feelings were much more violent than Ed's and she showed her anger. She got over it soon, provided she didn't have to repress it. Often she felt sorry for having exploded, and she would tell him she was sorry.

71

Ed believed that losing one's temper was a weakness which should never happen. This had always frustrated Eve. Fortunately, many years ago they had attended a series of classes at their church, on communications in marriage, and Ed realized it was not necessarily a flaw in Eve's character that occasionally she flew off the handle. Because Ed kept things in, Eve often misunderstood him and would get angry, whereupon he would feel very hurt and abused. It was also very difficult for him to acknowledge that he had been at fault and in their early years, he never said he was sorry. Gradually they began to understand each other better, and realized that even though they did not agree on everything they still loved each other. He learned to open up more. Their communication improved vastly over the years, and Eve's angry outbursts occurred less often. Although Ed never showed his anger, he would hurt inside. The more it hurt, the more control he would exert. He would seem uncaring and indifferent, which frustrated Eve. She wanted to get through Ed's mask. The final effect of Ed's bottling up was that he became physically ill.

When Eve learned this, she was more successful in avoiding open quarrels. In recent years they had had very few quarrels and had usually been able to articulate what was bothering them before a quarrel developed. But now it seemed that all the lessons learned over the years were forgotten. Eve was very angry because of her inability to reach Ed. He refused to enter into any discussion because he felt Eve was so unreasonable that he could not talk to her. Instead of making up before the night was far spent, as they usually did, the angry silence continued until later that night until Eve picked up her pillow, got a blanket, and went into the guest room.

They barely said a word the next morning at the breakfast table. They were both pale and haggard after a sleepless night. This was worse than anything that had ever occurred during their entire married life. Eve had expected her decision to break up their marriage to be painful, but she never imagined that she would feel this miserable. She had thought that they would separate as reasonable people. After all, they were still in love and should be able to continue as friends. Instead, they were tormenting each other as never before. In her agony Eve buried herself in her work. She had no idea how Ed was bearing it. Although they continued to share the same house, they treated each other as strangers. After a couple of weeks, Ed told her, "We can't continue like this. I don't know about you, but I can't take it anymore."

Eve was sure he was going to tell her that he was leaving her, and she blanched with apprehension as her heart began to race. Instead he said, "I love you too much to live without you, so I'm going to give up my dream of moving to a warmer climate to enjoy the remaining years of my life."

When Eve finally comprehended what Ed was saying she jumped up and ran sobbing into his arms. They held each other tightly as the tears ran down their cheeks.

"Don't think that this is easy for me," Ed said. "I'm giving up everything we had planned for so long. I hope you won't be sorry. I may not be around when you're ready to retire, and we won't be able to share all those wonderful things we talked about."

"It's only a few more years. We'll have many years together after that yet," Eve replied.

"I hope so. In the meantime, it's going to be pretty difficult for me. Now that summer is coming it won't be too bad, but I dread the winter. We'll just have to live a day at a time. I'll keep busy in the summer by working in the garden. I can start planning for that now."

"Oh, thank you so much. I'll make it up to you in other ways," Eve promised.

It was with great relief that she accepted Ed's decision. Her appetite improved immediately and once again she was able to sleep peacefully. Ed also seemed happy as he made plans for his summer plantings. On the surface, everything appeared fine again, but Eve had a small nagging feeling of guilt which she tried to bury. She plunged deeply into her work again, relieved that she could complete the many things she had started and eager to try new experiments. Yet deep down she wondered if she was right in accepting Ed's concession in order that she might continue her work.

CHAPTER NINE

Eve and Ed had often accompanied each other when one of them had to attend an out-of-town meeting. It had not always been possible because of their different commitments. Now Eve had a professional meeting scheduled for Friday evening and since she and Ed wanted to spend as much time together as possible, and he was now free to do so, he would come along. They decided to stay overnight at a motel, returning the next day, making a mini-vacation of the trip. She left the office a half-hour early and drove home for Ed. It would take them two hours to reach their destination and they'd need a little time before the dinner that preceded the meeting.

They sped along on the superb, divided highway, bypassing all the towns. Only a decade earlier, they remembered how this same road had been a bumpy, two-lane highway. Much of the charm of the old curving road had been sacrificed for efficiency and the countryside itself, with its gently rolling hills and woods, had receded. They read familiar names of towns on the exit lanes of the freeway. Now all the little towns were bypassed as they sped along. They had no desire to leave the highway to revisit localities which held nostalgic memories. They drove over a familiar river which now had two bridges for the divided highway, in place of the one bridge which had previously carried all the traffic. The familiar cottages and houses they had seen so often during their travels still remained on the banks of the river.

"At least there is no change here," commented Ed.

"I'm sure the people that live in them have changed, just as we and everything else have," replied Eve.

In no time at all it seemed, they reached their destination. Ed went to the motel desk to register, as Eve stood nearby. Suddenly he turned around with pen in hand and called out in a loud voice, "How shall I register us?"

Eve turned red as a beet. "Why Dr. and Mrs. Ed Wood, of course." She thought she noticed an amused look on the clerk's face. Did she and Ed appear to be an unmarried couple sharing a room? When they reached their room, she chided him for causing this embarrassment. "Why did you do such a silly thing?"

"How did I know what name you used when you registered for your meeting?"

"Dr. Hart, of course, but what has that to do with our motel registration?"

"Well, they might want to contact you, and how would they know you are Mrs. Wood. Mostly, you want to be known as Dr. Hart."

"In a situation like this, where we are together as a married couple, my profession does not enter the picture. It does present problems though, doesn't it, to have different names for a married couple? What I would really prefer would be to be called Dr. Eve Hart Wood, using my own family name as well as my acquired married name. They do this in some European countries, but here in this country it's either one or the other."

"You have a point there."

"After all, I did get my degree under my own name, and was known professionally by it long before I ever married you, so if there has to be a choice of one or the other, that's the name I usually prefer."

"That's what I thought," said Ed, "and that's why I was confused."

"Well, some stupid clerk would misinterpret it."

"Let's forget it now. We better get ready for the meeting," Ed said.

Eve and Ed had attended each other's meetings so often that their separate colleagues were no strangers to either of them. Ed quickly entered into conversations with Eve's colleagues, but when the lecture began, he started to show signs of being bored. Eve was apprehensive that he would show his boredom through repeated yawning. At least he didn't fall asleep.

After the meeting, they walked arm in arm back to the motel. The streets were deserted and the night air felt refreshing. They took deep breaths to rid their lungs of the tobacco smoke of one of their table companions. In recent years there had been much publicity on the dangers to health of smoking. At most medical meetings there was very little smoking anymore. However, an individual here and there still polluted the air around him. Some men had changed from cigarettes to pipe smoking but this was equally obnoxious to both Eve and Ed, and cigar smoke actually made her quite ill.

Ed suggested they try to name the stars, which were quite visible. Eve did her best, which was not very good. Ed, on the other hand, knew many of them and he rattled off their names.

They quietly made their way through the motel corridor to their room and retired.

Before leaving the motel they telephoned some friends to say hello. Mary and Ben urged them to drive over before returning home and have lunch with them. They had built a beautiful home for themselves, which Eve and Ed loved to visit. The new home was on the edge of a forest which provided a screen of privacy from the road below, as well as from neighbors behind the house. Mary and Ben took them out to the large-wooden platform porch built on to the house at the back. They gave them field glasses to do some bird watching, being great bird lovers themselves. Peering through the glasses they saw numerous bird feeders among the trees. Under the trees they saw water fountains and bird baths. There were birds all over the place. Some had wintered here, others had returned from their southern habitats.

"I wish I knew what all these birds were. I suppose you can name them all," Eve said.

"Pretty much so," Ben replied. "We keep our bird book nearby, so that if we see a strange bird we can identify it."

They were also great lovers of nature and had developed a near-paradise out of the rough, but fertile terrain. Spring flowers, such as daffodils, tulips and jonquils, were in profuse bloom. After strolling about and admiring the flowers, Eve and Ed went back to the porch to watch the birds, hear them call their mates and splash around in the water that had been set out for them. Mary, in the meantime, had been inside, preparing the lunch. She called them in. The table was set before the windows so they could continue to look out at the beautiful scenery and the birds.

"Are most of these vegetables from your own garden?" Eve asked.

"They're all from our garden, also the berries and fruit. I froze them and we've had enough to last all winter, in fact until our next crop comes in," Mary replied.

"Yes, we grow all our own food except for the meat, milk and grains," Ben explained.

"You're quite the gardener," Ed complimented.

"I enjoy it. I like to see things grow."

"And I enjoy preparing foods out of them," added Mary.

"I certainly envy you for what you're able to get out of the ground, in addition to all the beauty you have created here. I'm no gardener, but Ed grows flowers in our small garden. And now that he's retired, he has plans to grow some vegetables too," remarked Eve.

"You seem satisfied with your present way of life away from the cares of your former jobs," Ed suggested.

"Indeed we are!" Mary and Ben answered in chorus.

"Well, I'm afraid we'll have to leave now. It was such a pleasure to visit you," said Ed.

Eve repeated Ed's thanks and reluctantly they said good-by to their friends. As they sped along the highway again, Eve said, "This weekend jaunt has really been a refreshing mini-vacation. We should do it more often."

Ed agreed. For him it had been a bit of variety in a narrowing world. For Eve, it had prepared her to cope more easily with the challenges of the week ahead. She readily acknowledged that recreation had an important place in her life. After a long silence, Ed said, "There, you see, some people have made a success of their retirement."

"Hm! But they didn't leave their familiar hometown," was Eve's reply.

CHAPTER TEN

Eve was still sputtering as she told Ed about the meeting she had attended that afternoon with a group of women who had invited her to tell them about the work of her agency.

"They have no idea what the world is all about when they view it from their comfortable suburban homes with all the advantages that money and position can bring them."

"Start from the beginning so I can follow you," Ed interrupted.

"Well, here I was, telling them about the patients attending our clinics, when one of the women, wearing a deceptively simple dress which must have cost a fortune, just as her ring with a diamond like a huge rock must have, asked in a carefully modulated voice. . . ."

"Aren't you exaggerating a bit now about her appearance and what she wore?"

"Do you have to interrupt me all the time? Can't you see I'm angry enough already, without you adding steam to it?"

"I'm sorry. Go on."

"I don't much feel like saying anything anymore. I thought you would understand and back me up."

Ed got up and put his arms around her. "Please tell me. Don't be so touchy. Get it off your mind, it will help calm you down."

"O.K., but don't make anymore nasty remarks. Well, as I was saying, this woman asked me did our patients pay anything for their services, and if not how many were on welfare."

"What's wrong with that question?"

"There you go again! Just wait and hear what follows. I told her that since we were getting federal funds we couldn't charge for our services, but that we got reimbursed by the welfare department for their patients. She repeated her question about how many were on welfare. I told her about a third of the patients."

"What did she say to that?"

"With her smooth, silky voice, she said 'If only a third are on welfare, what pray, makes the others eligible for your

79

clinics?' I told her we had determined the area in the city that had the greatest number of poor people and that we had set up our clinics in these areas to serve the people. She asked why they didn't go to the private physicians and I said, because they couldn't afford it, and she had the nerve to tell me that we were taking patients away from the private physicians."

"Any time I go to my doctor, he is so busy he can't see me immediately," Ed remonstrated.

"That's what I told her too. Then she said her husband, who is a doctor, had told her that patients in public clinics get very poor care. I told her that is not the case in our clinics because we give the best care we know how and we were interested in all aspects that had a bearing on the patient's health and that we did a great deal of teaching on preventive health care through our nurses and other staff."

"Did that satisfy her?"

"No not really. She told me we have to be very careful that those who could afford private care would be screened out and not accepted at clinics. Then another older women very self-righteously declared that we were helping to swell the welfare rolls by condoning their laziness."

"What did she mean by that?" Ed asked.

"She told me that by coddling and accepting them, they had no desire to work when everything was handed to them on a silver platter. I explained that the majority of the poor on welfare rolls were the elderly, whom we of course did not see in our maternity, family planning and children's clinics. The others were mostly children without fathers in the home, or sick people. She refused to listen and expounded with great authority about how poor her parents had been but had worked hard and had never asked for help or been on welfare."

"I hope you told her that many of us came from poor homes as far as money was concerned."

"No, I didn't. She was so adamant in her own opinions there was no point in trying to change them. Oh, it makes me so mad I could scream. If they only would put themselves in the shoes of these people for even one day, they would have a better understanding."

"It's pretty difficult to understand when you're light miles away from the problem," Ed said.

"What can I do to change these people?" Eve cried out in great anguish.

"You're doing all you can, sweetheart," Ed consoled her.

"No, not half enough. I can't get the 'haves' to understand the plight of many of the poor."

"You can't be sure but maybe you did plant a seed of understanding among some of them," Ed replied.

"Maybe so, they weren't all that bad, in fact there were several of the younger women who supported me. And we have many cultured, wealthy women who work as volunteers in our clinics and are our best public relations people."

"There, you see, it isn't all so bleak. Don't take it so hard," Ed said.

"Hard! This is my life's work, it has to be of some use!"

"It must discourage you," Ed agreed.

"It makes me so frustrated when I can't seem to penetrate the thick wall of their ignorance. They even said that our programs were immoral, like the birth control services to single girls. On the one hand, they accused us of promoting out-of-wedlock pregnancies and swelling the welfare rolls, and then in the next breath, they're saying we should do nothing to prevent these pregnancies. You just can't win," Eve said in a tired voice.

"Neither you nor I can do anything about the views of the young people of today. It is difficult for older persons and many parents to accept the beliefs and actions of the younger generation," Ed commented.

"Yes, it is difficult for parents to be questioned by their offspring as to the validity of their mores when they have long ago established their own standards or follow the standards that were established for them regarding behavior and ideals," Eve nodded.

"I can understand why some older people want to move into retirement communities where there are only people of the same age and inclinations," Ed said.

"I guess today's meeting shows that I am really siding with the younger people and certainly the minorities and other under-privileged people. It must be pretty hectic for older people to defend their beliefs, but it must be hard for the younger generation too. You know, some of the standards of the middle-aged are pretty phony, and the young people can see through them," Eve pointed out.

81

"It is certainly more tranquil and peaceful when you don't have to defend your own views," Ed said.

"But that's what keeps you on your toes and makes you evaluate your own views," Eve countered. "I'm sure we stay more alert when we have to wrack our brains and we may even stay younger as a result of it."

"Let's forget the troubles of other people for awhile. All your days go into helping them or doing something on their behalf. Let's think of us now. Come on outside and see what I did today," Ed said, pulling Eve out of her chair.

They went out into the gathering dusk. The grass which such a short while ago had lain mottled with a covering of a greyish web had been raked clean.

"It looks so nice and clean," Eve remarked. "The grass has a chance to grow now."

The tulips were beginning to flower and the rhubarb was pushing forth leaves. To Eve's delight, the tiny blue flowers at the edge of the lawn at the back of the house were blooming in small clusters. They were as sure a sign of the approaching summer as were the robins that were still pecking at the ground in search of worms in spite of the increasing darkness.

Eve took Ed's arm and laid her head against his shoulder as they made their way back into the house.

CHAPTER ELEVEN

The light was peeking from around the curtains in the darkened bedroom when Eve opened her eyes. It was on the dot of eight, as it usually was on another of those precious Saturday mornings when the hated alarm clock was silent. On weekdays it rang out its urgent command at six, breaking the hold that sleep had on its willing subject. Eve wanted to know what the day was going to be like. She was usually depressed and sad on cloudy, rainy days and exuberant and joyful on sunny days. Ed's mood depended largely on Eve's. She nudged Ed gently and after he was sufficiently awake told him that it looked like a bright morning and she was sure it was going to be a good day. Ed arose and went to the windows. The shades went up with a snap, revealing a bright blue sky. Eve got up also and looked out. "It is nice, isn't it?" she remarked. Since is was such a beautiful morning and she felt happy, she tried to whistle as she did her regular morning exercises. Only a small squeak emerged. It had been so long ago when she as a child had seriously whistled — against the warnings of her old-fashioned grandmother, who said it was not ladylike and besides she was calling for the devil when she whistled.

In the meantime Ed had already put the coffee on, and when the delicious aroma drifted up the stairs she ran down to prepare the breakfast. As they sat at the table Ed handed her the binoculars and said, "Look up to the top branch of the bittersweet over the patio, and you'll see a robin singing his head off."

Eve took the glasses, and sure enough, after a little searching she was able to focus on the fluffy bird with its red breast. It was chirping at the top of its voice. Summer was almost here.

Before getting up from the table Eve asked Ed, "Don't you think it would be a good idea to have our morning devotions right after breakfast on weekends, when we have the time for it? My uncle and aunt used to do that every morning and I think it's a nice way to start the day."

"I agree with you," replied Ed, so Eve fetched the Bible

and started with the Book of Romans in the New Testament. Paul made heavy reading and occasionally Eve repeated a sentence to really grasp the meaning of the words. After she finished reading they bowed their heads and clasped each other's hands as Ed prayed. Surely the words of Jesus, "Where two or three are gathered together in my name, there am I with you," still rang true, even today. Eve was caught up with the feeling that the spirit of God was present and surrounded them with love and mercy. "This is surely the right way to start the new day." The Saturday morning chores had to be done first. With the inside chores done, Eve went outside to join Ed who was busy working up the ground around the roses and picking weeds. There was sound all around. The robins' song, the mourning doves' cooing, the hoarse chirp of the sparrows which had been around all winter and now were eagerly building nests, and the raucous sound of the blackbirds.

Eve picked a weed or two and swept off the walks, but mostly she watched and encouraged Ed in his work. After taking time out for lunch and resting for a while, they continued with the yard work. The sun was high and the air felt balmy and warm for early summer. Eve sat on the front steps and skimmed through the newspaper. She turned her face toward the sun and urged Ed to join her for a few minutes. It began to cool off in the late afternoon and Ed felt he had worked enough and was ready to go indoors. Eve felt a pleasant fatigue too, not so much from working but from the warmth of the sun and the relaxing. After a shower and rest, they felt greatly refreshed and were looking forward to a dinner invitation and visit with relatives of Eve's. It would be a treat not to have to prepare their own dinner.

Their social life was necessarily limited primarily to weekends. Mostly their friends were their family and relatives. The remainder of their social life revolved around their colleagues and club events. These included dinners, banquets, usually at some hotel, and cocktail parties.

It was still light when they drove to their dinner engagement. Traffic was light on the parkway and they drove slowly to enjoy the scenery along the way. The sun was close to the horizon when they reached their destination. Their hosts Roy and Kay, met them at the door and took their wraps. Then Kay went into the kitchen to put the finishing touches on the dinner, while Roy took them into the living room. They were the only guests, and could completely relax with their relatives.

Early on Monday morning Eve asked Bertha to arrange for a time for her and the agency health educator to meet with the new administrator for a group of loosely organized non-public schools to introduce themselves and to discuss with him the city-wide health meeting that Eve was planning to hold in the fall to acquaint personnel in these schools with health policies and regulations. After Bertha left, Eve sat quietly for a moment. She wondered how she would fare with the new administrator. Changes occurred so rapidly both in organization and personnel it was difficult to keep up. She hoped she could reach the school children ultimately, because all her efforts were for their health and well-being. Bertha informed Eve that everything was in order for her and her colleague to meet with the administrator of the new set-up in his office in the coming week.

At the appointed time Eve and her colleague arrived at his office and made their arrival known to his secretary. The secretary looked at the appointment calendar, shook her head and asked if they might not have made a mistake since she had no record of their meeting.

"Oh, there can't be a mistake, my secretary told me everything was in order for this meeting." Eve looked with dismay at her companion.

"Let me look in another book. Yes, I see here that instead of meeting with Mr. Samson, you are to meet with Mr. Adams who has been assigned to work with outside agencies on his behalf."

Eve and her companion glanced at each other with surprise. They were directed to wait for Mr. Adams in his office. Eventually he arrived with his coat tails flying. Immediately he told them, "I'm sorry I can give you only a few moments. I'm in a great hurry, because I have to appear shortly at a news conference. We're in the middle of a publicity campaign which is taking just about all our time."

Eve felt herself in a dither and wondered how she was going to get everything said. Mr. Adams's behavior was contagious. So she rushed on with a gush of words, "We came here to meet the administrator and get his support for the school health meeting we are planning for next fall."

Mr. Adams was rummaging through his desk, but looked up to say, "Oh, Mr. Samson has authorized me to tell you that you have our full support, just go ahead and do what you think needs to be done."

"Well, we'd like to acquaint your principals and other personnel of the school systems with preventive health measures that schools can undertake to keep both students and teachers well."

"Fine, fine! Just tell them what you want, and if you have trouble getting your message across, let me know and I'll see to it that it gets done," Mr. Adams assured her.

"We can't be that autocratic. We want to have a meeting with them so they would have an opportunity to react, and ask questions," explained Eve.

Mr. Adams replied, "Prepare a directive to the schools, telling them what the health agency expects of them."

"But we don't want to do it that way. I would like to have a fall health meeting, for your principals and teachers, such as we have for the parochial schools every year. But we can't do it unless Mr. Samson notifies the schools about the meeting and urges staff to attend."

At that moment there was a knock at the door. The secretary stuck her head in and announced that the photographers and reporters had arrived. Mr. Adams rose and told Eve, "Go ahead and arrange things as you want to," and rushed out of the room.

Eve and her companion were flabbergasted. "Why, he didn't hear a word I said!" sputtered Eve. "My words washed over him like water off a duck."

They left, feeling frustrated and slighted. Outside the door they met a gentleman who introduced himself as Mr. Samson who told them, "My secretary informed me you were meeting with Mr. Adams. I'm sorry I haven't time to meet with you myself, but I have assigned Mr. Adams to be my liaison with all outside agencies dealing with our schools. I hope you were able to accomplish your mission."

Eve and her companion left the building with dragging steps. "I've never felt so let-down in all my life. We not only were not able to meet with Mr. Samson, but even his deputy gave us the brush-off. I feel like a squashed fly." After a while, and more calmly, Eve continued, "I suppose we accomplished half of what we came here for."

"What's that? I don't think we accomplished anything."

"Mr. Samson did introduce himself to us and at least he knows what agency we represent. That's one reason why we came here. We'll have to think how we'll accomplish the second half," Eve said.

Her thoughts raced ahead of her. "I suppose we could hold the orientation meeting right in our own building. Then it would be our meeting, and we would be completely responsible for it and wouldn't have to bother Mr. Samson with it at all."

"You mean Mr. Adams, don't you?"

"We'd still have to clear it with the school officials and see if they will send a notice in their news bulletin to the schools," Eve mused.

"You're awfully optimistic."

"Sometimes yes, sometimes no. This time I still think things will work out. They seemed under great pressure in that office, so they must feel they have greater priorities right now than our health meeting. Mr. Samson seemed like a nice enough person. I wish we had direct contact with him, though. It's going to be rather difficult to work with Mr. Adams."

"You said it!" replied her colleague.

In order to put the day's frustrations out of her mind, when Eve got home that evening she suggested to Ed that they go out to eat at the quaint, cozy restaurant across the river from them and near the shopping center. Ed agreed, and off they drove. There were many young families with children present, and also older persons who lived in a retirement complex close by. Eve marvelled at the courteous treatment afforded these older persons by the young waitresses. Some of the elderly seemed to have trouble hearing so the waitresses made every effort to speak clearly, bending down close to the hearing aides which many wore. They were just as helpful to the parents with young children. All in all it was a comfortable, home-like atmosphere. In this environment it was easy for Eve to put aside her thoughts of work. She remembered the Bible saying, paraphrased in her own words: "Sufficient to the day are its own problems. Tomorrow would take care of itself."

CHAPTER TWELVE

It was the most beautiful time of the year. The air was clear. The green of the trees was pure and the lawns around homes were immaculate rugs of green velvet. Roses were blooming profusely. As soon as Eve arrived home from work she called to Ed, "Let's go to the lake for a swim. Who wants to stay indoors on a day like this?"

Ed was agreeable, "Yes, let's go. It'll be refreshing."

"Shall we take a picnic supper, or return home to eat?" Eve asked.

"Why don't we just go for our swim and eat later, at home? We could take some crackers and cheese along to hold us over until we get back," Ed replied. They put on their bathing suits under their slacks and shirts, packed the newspaper in the tote bag along with the crackers, cheese and a soft drink. They also put a couple of blankets in the trunk of the car and drove off. They parked their car under a tree on the roadway circling the lake and laid the blankets on the ground a couple of yards from the water.

"I'll beat you to the lake," Eve cried out as she rushed into the water. Ed followed at a more leisurely pace. He grimaced as he threw water on his arms and chest, "Whew! It's cold." Then he swam toward Eve who was some distance away. They gradually warmed up and Eve called out to Ed, "It's not cold at all anymore."

"It's better, but for the first swim of the season, I don't think I'll overdo it," replied Ed. He swam a few more turns and went into the sun to dry himself. Eve stayed in a bit longer but soon she followed Ed. They sat down on plastic pillows so as not to wet the blankets and waited for the sun and warm air to dry their suits. Ed became immersed in the newspaper while Eve stared at the water. The lake shimmered in the sunshine. She counted at least twenty sailboats on the water. Children were swimming nearby under the supervision of their parents. The air reverberated with their joyful laughter and screams. Music from portable radios drifted towards them. Many people were sunning themselves just as Eve and Ed were doing. The breeze from across the lake was refreshing, and the city streets seemed far away. They stayed at the lake until the sun nearly set. New groups of people were coming out to the lake for their picnic suppers, laying out their things on the grass. Eve prepared a simple supper at home. After a while she noticed that Ed was unusually quiet. He never was a great talker, but after the joyous time at the lake it seemed strange that he should be so withdrawn. His cheeks seemed flushed but Eve attributed it to the effects of the sun. After a while he stopped eating, saying he had no appetite. Eve asked him, "Is something bothering you? Aren't you well?"

Without answering, he got up from the table and soon Eve heard him rummaging in the bathroom overhead. She continued to eat although the food seemed to stick in her throat with her growing apprehension. After a short time Ed came down and announced to Eve, "My temperature is elevated."

"Do you have any other symptoms? Is your throat sore, are you developing a cold? Or do you have diarrhea?" Eve reached for Ed's wrist to check his pulse. It was fast.

"No, I don't feel anything but I feel hot and tired," Ed replied.

"You better get up to bed. Maybe you caught a little cold sitting in your wet trunks. You'll probably feel better tomorrow." She went upstairs with Ed and prepared the bed. "I guess I'd better get right to sleep, I feel tired enough," he said.

Eve went into the adjoining room so as not to disturb him. She tried to read but had difficulty concentrating. From time to time he asked for some water and later in the evening he wanted her to take his temperature again. It was about the same as earlier.

"Make a record of my temperatures and pulse rate and when I first fet ill," Ed requested.

"O.K. I'll do it," Eve assured him.

During the night he perspired heavily and by morning his fever had abated. Eve felt she could go to work since Ed felt better. "You'll have to stay in bed though," she told him.

She placed the telephone next to the bed so he could call her if he needed to. She also placed a water pitcher on the bedside table.

"I'll come home at noon to prepare lunch for us. Are you comfortable now, and can I leave you?" she asked.

90

"You just go on to work, I'll manage just fine here," he told her.

At the office Eve was busy so her mind was not on Ed all the time. She called a couple of times to see how he was. He assured her there was no need for her to come home before lunch. At noon she found him reading a book in bed. She took his temperature and found it was a little higher than in the morning, but nothing alarming. "You wouldn't expect it to disappear immediately," she told him. When Eve came home after work she found Ed flushed again, and his temperature raised. There were no other symptoms and Ed did not seem very ill.

"We'll just have to wait it out. It should go away," Ed was hopeful. So each morning Eve settled him for a day in bed while she went to work, returning each noon to prepare a lunch for both of them. It was necessary for her to curtail some of her activities, such as out-of-town commitments and all of her noon meetings. Otherwise, her work went on as usual. The fever continued day after day. Ed developed heavy night sweats necessitating a change of pajamas a couple of times during the night, but there were no other symptoms. Finally, by Saturday morning when the fever had not abated, but each succeeding day had gone just a little higher than the day before, Eve could no longer contain her worries.

"I can't carry the responsibility for your illness any longer. I'm going to call your doctor," she told Ed.

"I don't want you to call him. He'll make me go to the hospital and I'm not going," Ed declared.

"But I can't take care of you. I have no way of doing any tests on you. I haven't the slightest idea what is wrong with you."

"Please don't call him," Ed pleaded. He looked apprehensive and unhappy.

"Sweetheart, it's for your own good. I want you well soon, and the only way that can be done is to find out what ails you so you can be treated."

Reluctantly Ed gave his permission. "We'll see what he has to say."

Ed was right. The physician did indeed order him into the hospital immediately. Ed became flustered and quite upset. He got up from bed saying, "I've got to wash up and shave so

91

I'll be presentable."

"Don't rush around like that. I'll help you with clean clothes and I'll pack a suitcase for you if you'll only tell me what you want. Don't over-exert yourself, take your time when you clean up," Eve put her arms around Ed to calm him down. He appeared quite weak as she helped him down the stairs and into the car. Her heart went out to him as she said, "In no time at all you'll be home again, and of course I'll spend every spare moment with you in the hospital." Eve drove Ed to the hospital and saw that he was settled in his room. They had decided on a double room because they hoped his stay at the hospital would be a short one. The other bed was fortunately vacant and remained so for the entire weekend. Since it was the weekend, only routine tests were done, none of which showed any clue to Ed's problem or the cause for his continuing fever. The doctor did a preliminary examination and said he would order more tests on Monday.

"See? I should have stayed at home at least until Monday," Ed grumbled.

"It was much easier for me to bring you here today, when I'm off work. Besides, you'll be all ready for your tests first thing Monday morning," Eve replied.

"You just wanted to get rid of me."

"What nonsense! I love you and I want you better as fast as possible. I'm not going to leave you except to go home to sleep," Eve reassured him.

She settled herself into the easy chair next to the window and right beside his bed. When Ed slept or read she was quiet, and when Ed was ready for company she carried on a quiet conversation with him. Gradually he resigned himself and calmed down. Every time he woke up from a sleep, he wanted reassurance that she was still there.

"I won't leave you without telling you, sweetheart," she told him, holding his hand in hers. She helped Ed with his food when they brought his tray in. He wasn't very hungry.

"For tomorrow you can order foods that are more to your liking," Eve told him as she helped him fill out the order form for the next day's meals.

"You better get some food yourself," Ed said. She went to the desk for permission to eat in the employees' cafeteria. She wasn't very hungry, but tried to do justice to the food

92

which was quite good. It was dark before Ed finally consented to Eve's leaving. She kissed him goodnight and said she would call as soon as she got home. Her thoughts were troubled as she drove home. The house seemed so quiet. Before going to bed she cleaned up the bedroom which had been left rather cluttered after their abrupt departure to the hospital. "Was it really only this morning that we left? It seems like a long time ago," she mused to herself.

It was a lonely night. Eve had difficulty getting to sleep in the bed that seemed so large now that she was occupying it alone. She heard every creak and snap of the house as she lay awake. In the morning she was tired from her useless vigil. She scolded herself, "Stupid, you can't help Ed or yourself when you're so tired. You'll have to learn to sleep alone. Worrying isn't going to help either."

She spent the next day, Sunday, at the hospital again much the same way as the day before, but left for home earlier since Monday was a working day. Monday morning established a sort of routine life for Eve. Soon after she arrived at the office, she telephoned him to see what kind of a night he had had.

"I slept well enough, but I perspired at night again," he said.

"Did you have the nurse change your pajamas?"

"No, I didn't want to bother them," he replied.

In an exasperated voice Eve admonished him, "But that's what they are there for!"

The remainder of the day was spent in the usual daily round of activities. Right after work she went home for a bite to eat and then rushed over to the hospital to spend the evening with Ed. He seemed happy to have her there but hated to see her leave.

"I told the nurses today to put up a sign that I didn't want any visitors besides you," he told her.

"Why don't you want visitors?"

"I'm too tired to talk with them."

Ed was alone for one more night, but the next day he had a roommate. This elderly man was a stroke victim who needed constant attention. Eve admired the wife who was with her husband from early morning till late at night. Ed told her that she fed her husband, turned him from side to side, listened to his garbled speech and seemed to understand what he was saying. The wife of this patient and Eve often went down together for their dinner and shared their concerns over their husbands. Once, when the wife was away for a while, one of their adult daughters with her own daughter came to the hospital. When they saw that their mother and grandmother was not there they sat down to wait for her. They talked to each other, completely ignoring the patient, just as though he did not exist or did not understand them. After a while they said they would leave because the mother had not arrived. Eve felt sorry for the poor man.

She quietly said to Ed, "That man's wife is certainly one of the unsung heroes of the world. I wonder if her family recognizes her worth and her sacrifices. That is what the marriage vow must mean, when it says 'for better or for worse, in sickness and in health'."

The days of Ed's hospital stay stretched to weeks, then a month and still there was no end in sight. The cause of his illness had not been determined and he was no better. Test after test was done. Nothing definitive turned up. So many blood specimens were collected that Ed was becoming anemic. Almost every morning he had to skip his breakfast for still another test. He was losing weight.

Eve was becoming very discouraged and worried night and day. He was wasting away before her eyes. She could tell that he was also worried, but both put on as brave a front as possible. Eve began to study her medical books for possible clues and spoke to her colleagues at the university to see if they could offer suggestions. She telephoned the health officer of the state where they had spent their winter vacation to see if Ed might harbor some strange infection contracted while they had been in the desert. Nothing.

CHAPTER THIRTEEN

Ed was now in a private room. His hospital stay had extended beyond all reason and the sight of the helpless man in the other bed had been much too discouraging. It was impossible to know how much longer Ed would have to remain, or indeed, if he would ever recover. But that was something Eve did not dare say aloud. In the quiet of the night the mournful thought occurred with increasing frequency. Ed did not say much anymore. He was very tired from the daily fevers and night sweats. It was pathetic to watch him get out of bed and take a few slow steps around the room, "So I won't lose all my muscle strength." Eve tried not to cry while she was with him.

One evening he was given a trial dose of a drug for his irregular heart beat. He began to complain of chills and asked for more covers and a hot water bottle for his cold feet. Eve rang for the nurses. She was ready to hit the ceiling when she was told the nurse could not get the hot water bottle without the permission of the resident doctor on call at the hospital. "Get him then!" Eve ordered.

The chills grew worse, so bad in fact, that Ed was visibly shaking, and the bed with him. Eve again frantically called the nurse and told her to call Ed's physician. A laboratory technician came in to take yet another blood specimen.

"This is a fine time to stick him again," Eve cried out.

"We have orders to do this in case of a chill," was the answer.

Eve no longer felt like a doctor. She was only a suffering and frantic wife. She cradled Ed in her arms trying to control his shaking. She held the covers tightly around him to warm him, as the blood was being drawn from the veins in his arm. After what seemed like an eternity, his shivers gradually decreased. Eve felt his pulse. It was extremely fast and thready. The nurse took his temperature and left the room with a serious look on her face. Eve ran after her, "What is it?"

The nurse seemed reluctant to tell her and merely said, "It's high."

Eve told her, "I'm a physician and I want to know how high it is."

Eve's heart leapt up into her throat when she heard what it was. It was much higher than the temperature of an adult should ever be, without very serious consequences. She went back into Ed's room. He was sleeping a jerky, restless sleep. There was nothing she could do. She could only pray and leave his care in the hands of God and Ed's physicians. She was prepared to spend the entire night with him, but the hospital staff persuaded her to go home and get some sleep. The nurse told her, "We have instructions from the doctor. If there should be any change we'll call you. We won't leave him alone."

Eve left the hospital reluctantly. She wanted to be with Ed in case he woke up and needed her. She was in the depths of despair. Ed was getting worse and there seemed no more hope. The cause of his trouble remained a mystery. She felt completely deserted by everyone. There was no one to whom she could turn for help. Her closest relatives, Roy and Kay, were off on vacation and she did not know where Ed's sons were. In her desperation she went to her next-door neighbors whom she knew in a friendly, superficial way and told them, "My husband is very ill and I might be called back to the hospital during the night. Would you please go with me if they do call?"

The man answered, "Well, of course. I'll tell my wife. Why don't you stay the night at our house?"

"No, I have to be at home so they can reach me if necessary."

She went back into her lonely house. She knelt beside her bed and prayed with great anguish that God would heal Ed, but if that were not His will, that He would give her strength for whatever ordeal she had to face. And to please let her know that she was not alone. To bear this burden alone was more than she could take. With the tears streaming down her cheeks she got up and prepared for bed. She had barely settled herself down when the telephone rang. "Oh, dear God no!" she cried out. But it was not the hospital. It was Ed's older brother calling from his home in Canada. "We just got home from our vacation and your letter telling us of Ed's illness was waiting for us here. I've tried to call you several times this evening but there was no answer. How is Ed?"

Eve replied, "He's very ill." She went on to describe his condition, speaking with great difficulty because she had trouble keeping sobs out of her voice.

Ed's brother told her, "We will leave from here by car tomorrow afternoon and should arrive there in a couple of days. In the meantime know that we are praying for Ed and for you."

Eve told him his call was already an answer to a prayer. "I was so alone, I didn't think I could carry the burden any longer by myself." She went back to bed, no less worried, but with the reassurance that she was not alone in her worries and sorrow. In the morning she returned to the hospital fearing the worst. Ed was very weak but he seemed better than he had the night before. He had slept and he had had no more chills. The doctor came in and said he would take Ed off all medications, since his reaction to a drug had been so severe the night before. But more tests were continued. Eve called the office to tell them she would not be in. She was too tired for one thing, she couldn't bear to leave Ed and she would have accomplished nothing at work. She didn't tell Bertha how very sick Ed was.

Ed's brother and sister-in-law arrived and stayed with her. They visited Ed in the hospital but the visits were limited to fifteen minutes twice a day. They stayed in the lounge while Eve was in the room with him. Eve just sat there, holding Ed's hand. No words were needed. Her presence was reassuring to Ed. After three days the visitors departed. The crisis seemed over and they did not want to be a burden for Eve. The evening before they left, Eve began to sob from sheer exhaustion and worry. Her sister-in-law put her arms around Eve and told her to just cry her fears away, it would help.

Very slowly Ed began to improve. His temperatures did not go as high as before, and his night sweats lessened. He had been off all medication for over a week, but the tests still continued. The doctors were determined to find a diagnosis. It began to seem that the after-effects of the tests were now worse than the illness they were trying to uncover. Eve and Ed were convinced that everything had been due to Ed's developing intolerance to the many drugs he had been taking under his doctor's orders over the years. It could also be that the drugs were having an adverse effect on each other. They discussed this with their physician but were not able to convince him. As far as he was concerned the diagnosis was, and remained "Fever of Unknown Origin." In any case now that Ed was off all drugs he was improving.

Eve returned to work after Ed seemed out of danger. His illness had taken its toll on her. She was constantly tired and had lost her zest for new challenges. The best she could hope for was to get through the day, but the pressures at work did not let up. She wished she could just sleep for a whole month, but this was not to be. Her time continued to be divided between office, hospital and nights at home.

Kay and Roy had returned from their vacation and asked Eve what they could do for her. She suggested, "If you could have me over for Sunday dinners it would give me a little variety. Just so I wouldn't have to stay long and visit." They understood that she had to get back to the hospital as soon as possible. So after this she went to their home for dinner on Sundays, for as long as Ed still remained at the hospital.

Eve had gone to church only once during Ed's long illness with Ed's brother and sister-in-law, but she felt lonely without Ed. She felt hurt because nobody asked about Ed, nobody even noticed that he was not with her. The church was too large for any intimacy among its thousands of members. Instead, she stayed at home and listened to an early Sunday morning church service over the radio before she drove off to the hospital. She felt better this way and could commune with God just as well in the quiet of her home as among a lot of strangers who nodded to her in church but had no knowledge of her personal life.

A few weeks later the doctor said Ed could go home on a day's leave to see how he stood it. Right after breakfast on a Sunday, Eve came for him. He was brought by wheelchair to the car and helped in. He looked so weak and thin Eve felt tears rising to her eyes. She drove slowly so Ed could absorb the sights around him and make the ride easier for him. Eve had fixed the living room couch as a bed for Ed. He was so happy to be home again, if even for just a visit. He walked around the rooms slowly, looking at this object and that and touching them caressingly. He rested, but was loathe to sleep which would waste the precious time allotted him to be at home. All too soon the leave was over, and Ed had again to be returned to the hospital in time for dinner. He had stood the trip very well and soon, God willing, he would come home for keeps.

That day finally dawned. Ed was bundled up for the ride home. It was a cloudy, dreary day, and there was a strong wind. Eve wanted to take no chances, so Ed was dressed warmly and she had heated up the car. A nurse pushed his wheelchair to the car, with Eve walking alongside him. Two aides followed with his suitcase and the plants he was taking home. Although Ed had had very few visitors during his long stay, he had been generously remembered with cards and flowers by family and associates.

In no time they were home together again. It was a strange feeling, as though they had been on a long trip and would have to get reacquainted with everyday life. Ed was very tired after the exhausting experience of preparing for the departure from the hospital. Eve helped him as he slowly climbed the stairs to the upstairs bedroom. He was glad to get into the bed he had left so long ago.

CHAPTER FOURTEEN

Ed was still too weak to stay at home alone. Eve took a couple of days off to stay with him, but tried to make other arrangements. Her work was beginning to suffer because of her previous absences, and her capacity for work had decreased because of the strain of Ed's long ordeal and her own total exhaustion. She tried to get a young student friend to stay with Ed. She told him, "You could do your studying in the next room. I just want somebody to be in the house in case Ed needs anything. You don't have to do anything for him. I'll even come home to make lunch for the two of you." But the young friend did not think Ed was ill enough for him to go to the trouble of driving all the way through town just to sit with him. He thought it was rather ridiculous. He refused to come. Finally, when she talked her problem over with the lady next door, this kind woman offered to come over. She was a nurse and was just now working the late evening shift and could well sit for a few hours with Ed. "I don't think it will be necessary for more than a week. Ed is gradually getting his strength back and can take care of his own personal needs," Eve told her.

Ed was determined to increase his strength by continuing the program of exercise he had started at the hospital, with no prodding from his physician. This consisted of short walks in the house from room to room. At first he avoided the stairs. When he came downstairs in the morning he did not go up again until evening. He rested on the living room couch. Gradually he stayed up longer and longer, doing mild exercises. The cough he had developed in the hospital continued to bother him at home. Eve bought him some toy balloons and told him to blow on them as hard as he could.

"I don't think you have been breathing deeply enough, having been on your back for so long," she told Ed. So he began blowing on the balloons and as they popped and broke, she bought more of them. This seemed to help because his troublesome cough was being reduced. Eventually Ed started taking short walks on the driveway behind the house. He ventured out when the weather was mild, and not

101

too hot. On rainy days, he had to forego his outside walk, but stepped all the more briskly indoors. As summer turned into fall Ed was walking around the block. But more and more he had to stay indoors as the weather grew colder and the skies became dark and cloudy. The cold air caused breathing difficulties for Ed just as before his illness. Although there was no recurrence of his illness, he had spells of weakness and dizziness. His anemic condition improved very slowly. The dizziness was more difficult to handle. He could not trust himself to drive the car yet, and of course, was completely dependent on Eve for transportation.

They spent their evenings quietly at home but ventured for short visits to see Roy and Kay. They themselves had only one or two persons at a time to the house to see Ed, including their sons. Any lengthy conversation drained Ed of his limited strength. Eve's spirits had risen considerably after Ed began to improve, and especially after he came home. But she was not able to rid herself of her apprehensions concerning him. She continued to be very tired. After all she was carrying a double load and still performing the chores Ed usually had done before his illness. She did his bank errands for him, paid the bills, and did all the food shopping. Ed did not dare to mingle among groups of people in shopping centers yet, because of the danger of exposing himself to infections.

Eve had also lost her zest at the office. She dreaded problems and delayed starting new plans. She delegated as many of her responsibilities as possible to others. She was sure time would heal her lassitude. But worst of all were her guilt feelings. It was clear that Ed would continue to have difficulty coping with the severe winters of the north. She remembered how he had said several times, "Maybe I won't be here to enjoy retirement with you if you wait much longer." It nagged at her mind. She had almost lost him. Now she had another chance, which is not given to all people. What was she going to do with it? It was obvious that Ed was bored with staying indoors so much. Although he didn't say anything, Eve knew that he was lonely at home, and eagerly awaited her return from work each evening. He began to take over some of the household chores. His health seemed so fragile yet that Eve was frightened anything might upset it. If only they lived in a warmer climate.

Eve was becoming convinced, however reluctantly, that her career was not the most important thing in life if it interfered with her personal relationships. She had previously agreed with a friend of hers, a career-woman who in middle age had just begun to climb the ladder, who had said, "I gave my time and years to our children when they were young. Now they are on their own, and it's my turn to develop myself in my profession. From now on, my husband will have to fit his life to mine. If my career takes me to Australia, he will just have to come along."

There were situations such as the one Eve found herself in where the husband's sacrifice was too great. Ed had already given up several years when he could have enjoyed a more leisurely life of retirement in a more pleasant environment. But he had chosen to work so she could continue with the work she had so loved. Later he had arrived at the place where he could work no longer. Now he was actually sacrificing his life to accommodate Eve. This was too much for Eve to accept. She loved him too much. His illness had brought the realization that her life was tied to Ed's more than she had ever imagined. They could never be like the couple who had jobs away from each other, and lived apart, only seeing each other at those times when one or the other could commute.

Eve reached the decision that Ed was more important to her than her job. The difficult phase she had just gone through had changed her values and priorities. The person who needed her most was right by her side, and not the anonymous public somewhere on the outside. The gratitude in Ed's eyes when she sat by him was more satisfying than all the accolades she could possibly receive from others. She knew what she had done in her profession would soon be forgotten when others took her place, but the love she and Ed had for each other would last till the end of their days. A new line of communication opened up between them, just as earlier in their lives when they were sharing both home and work experiences. No longer did she keep her fears and apprehensions to herself as when she had decided to continue to work, without discussing with Ed the reasons she had arrived at this decision. Each evening they discussed the happenings of that day. Eve made a special effort to relate to Ed the humorous events at work. They needed a little laughter to dispel the gloom of the past months. One evening they got down to serious discussion again.

"Ed, I'd be willing to give up my job to be with you and go wherever you want to, but I'm so scared of retirement," Eve said quietly.

"What are you scared of?"

"It seems to me that retired people are treated as though they aren't very important anymore. No one asks for their opinions. They're 'has beens.'"

"Is that how you yourself consider them?" Ed asked.

"In a way, yes. When a retired staff person comes to the office to see us, I tend to make the encounter as short as possible."

"I can understand that. The retired person has grown away, or perhaps it would be more correct to say the active staff have not remained in the same place, and so their paths have diverged," Ed replied.

"But I feel as though my life would be over if I gave up my profession," Eve countered. "It seems as though I have just gotten started in my work. Is this how short it is to be?"

"You would have different interests if you retired," Ed suggested.

"Yes, filling in my time with crafts, dabbling in painting and the like. I've never been interested in that kind of activity," Eve cried out.

"There would be other things to do."

"Like what? Cooking, cleaning the house? Is that what I got my medical education for, to clean out bathrooms? No thanks!"

"You wouldn't have to leave your intellectual pursuits behind," Ed retorted a little impatiently.

"Join a book review club? I'd rather read by myself and analyze my reading by myself."

"Sweetheart, you've always been yourself and different from many other women. I wouldn't expect you to act like other retirees. Although it seems to me you can't categorize all retirees into the same group. They're surely as different as they were in their active years."

Eve glanced at him. "I guess I'm being awfully ungrateful. I have you, and I guess we can think up something worthwhile for me to do."

"I need you more than you can imagine. My life isn't

worth anything if I can't share it with you," Ed said softly.

"I know, and the same holds true for me. It's just a matter of determining how we would share this new kind of life together. We can't just sit and do nothing together," Eve replied.

"We can make trips more often, and for longer periods. We can cultivate new friends, join some interesting clubs," Ed suggested.

"And sleep longer in the mornings without the alarm clock awakening us. All very good, but what would be the purpose of my life?" Eve demanded.

"I can't answer that for you. You'd have to determine that yourself. You've spent your entire professional life in service to others. I would think you would continue to do that in a different way, in a new setting," Ed replied.

"I guess you're right. I wouldn't allow myself to be molded into the form that people expect a retired person to be. You've always supported me in being creative and useful. If I could just look at it in the way that I am giving up one job to go into something else," Eve said.

"That's the right attitude," Ed said.

"If I only knew what I was going into, I'd feel better," Eve said.

"Knowing you, I am sure you would never be content just to stay at home or get involved in any social whirl. Certainly opportunities will present themselves in whatever location we move to. You could participate in community activities, if in no other way, at least in a volunteer capacity," Ed reassured Eve.

"Yes, I guess so. The most important thing is not to neglect you, and make you unhappy in the process," Eve replied,

"And for you to get personal satisfaction," Ed continued.

"Let's sleep on it now," Eve suggested.

"Good idea. Let's go up to bed, I'm tired already," Ed said.

The next evening they examined other aspects of retirement.

"You know, it might be fun to go to a new location. We've always had a spirit of adventure. Here you came from Canada in middle age to start a new career, and I did likewise, leaving familiar faces and places behind when I came here to accept my job," Eve said.

"No, we're not afraid of new experiences. It was even rather courageous of me to marry you," Ed stated.

"What do you mean by that?" asked Eve.

"You were a well-established career woman when I married you. I was sure you were set in your ways, and probably quite domineering in your attitudes. I wasn't sure how we could meld our lives together," Ed answered with a smile.

"Don't think it was easy for me to adjust to marriage and a ready-made family," Eve in turn explained.

"We made the jump in faith and look how well it all turned out. Let's jump in faith again, trusting everything will turn out for the best," Ed said.

"One thing I must insist on," said Eve.

"What?" asked Ed.

"I refuse to say that I'll retire. I can't stand the word 'retirement.' I'll tell people and that's the way I think about it myself, that I'm quitting my work because *you're* retired and can't tolerate the cold winters up here anymore," Eve said.

"That's O.K. with me, although I don't know why you can't say that you took an early retirement," Ed said.

"No, it's resigning or I will continue to work," Eve threatened.

"O.K., O.K., don't get so excited," Ed assured her.

"Now that we've dispensed with that, let's get back to more important decisions. You and I know now that I'll give up my job. But I don't want any one to know about it yet. We have so much to think about first, and plan how we're going to go about it," Eve said.

"It suits me," Ed replied. Already he had a look of relief on his face as he came to kiss Eve and take her in his arms.

CHAPTER FIFTEEN

"One of the first things I'll have to do," Eve told Ed, discussing their plans, "is to notify the health officer of my intentions so he can find my successor."

"Good idea," agreed Ed. "What should our timetable be?"

"Well, let's see. We can't sell our house overnight. I have to pull together odds and ends at the office, such as the year-end annual report, budget for next year and other things."

"We'll have to do minor repairs in the house before we put it on the market," Ed said.

"Maybe you can put daubs of paint in places where it has chipped off, like in the bathrooms and kitchen. Fortunately we had a major remodeling job of painting and wallpapering done a couple of years ago, so things are not in too bad a shape," Eve replied.

"And the outside was overhauled only five years ago and is in excellent shape," Ed continued.

"O.K. How does right after the first of the year sound to you as the time we would have everything wound up and could be on our way?" Eve asked.

"Sounds reasonable to me," Ed agreed.

"So here's the timetable, at least tentatively," Eve said. "I'll talk to the health officer at the first opportunity. But I don't want my staff to know yet. It will be difficult to get things done at the office if they know too much in advance. You may need two or three weeks to do the minor repairs around here. And maybe you could contact the real estate agent up there in the mountains that we met when we were on our vacation at the beginning of this year," Eve suggested.

"You did like the area and the places he showed us and are satisfied that that is where we would go?" Ed wanted to be sure.

"I can't think of a better place and when we were there, we did say that if ever the time came for moving that would be it," she assured him.

At the first opportunity Eve made an appointment with the health officer to make her announcement. His reaction was, "I was afraid of this. I was only hoping it wouldn't occur until after my time. Ever since Ed's illness I've been anticipating this moment. How am I going to replace you? Do you have any replacement in mind?" he asked her.

"I have two or three persons in mind. Civil Service, of course, will have to make the choice, but I would hope it could be someone from my own department. This person would already know many things, so the job of orienting would not be so overwhelming as starting with a new person from the outside," Eve said.

"Why don't you talk to them and see if someone would be interested?"

"I'll do that and let you know. I would prefer not to have this matter of my leaving become public as yet. I would like to make the announcement to my staff myself in due time, if that is agreeable with you," Eve said. It was, and so the matter was left for the time being. The die was cast, but that did not mean that Eve was able to accept the decision with no further thought or backward glance. Many a night, when Ed was sleeping peacefully beside her, Eve would wake up with a deep sense of loss.

"My God, what have I done? My life is over already and it has hardly begun." She would weep into her pillow in the dark of the night, trying to be quiet so Ed would not wake up. She felt she was betraying herself. In the morning her fears of the night would recede as she became involved in the practical details of the day. She contacted the full-time physicians in her department and told them, "My husband and I have decided that we must move to a warmer climate because of his health. For this reason I must resign my position."

"Oh, surely not!"

"Yes, I'm afraid so. That's the reason I wanted to talk to you to tell you my position will eventually be open."

They were silent for a moment, then one replied, "It will be hard to replace you. I would have to talk to my family first before I could make any decision, either pro or con." The others echoed her words.

"Yes, of course. We should keep this information to ourselves. I don't want the rest of the staff to know about it yet. If any of you are interested in the job there is a lot of red tape to be cleared first before the position is opened. The health officer, of course, knows about my decision already." She went on, "The job description will need to be revised. It's been many years since that was last done. Many new responsibilities have been added to my job since then."

"I don't think anyone could take all the responsibility you are now carrying, on a short notice," was the remark of one of them.

"Oh, I'm sure my successor would grow into the job as he gets to know it," said Eve. "In case a qualified person is found within the agency, Civil Service might make the job promotional so there would be no competition from the outside." They parted with the understanding that they would talk to their families, and also reassured her that they would tell no one until after Eve made the announcement to her staff.

The days flew by. Eve was caught up in the activities at home as well as at the office. She continued with the ordinary tasks at hand and those relating to her leaving. Another year had passed since Eve's last birthday. Not only that but she would pass into the next decade. The thought was disturbing, but as she told Ed, "To borrow a phrase 'what was the alternative?' "

She did not regret the years that had passed. Each phase in her life had brought joys as well as sorrows.

But Ed had brought so much happiness into her life. Until his retirement and recent illness, she had to occasionally pinch herself to assure herself that she was not dreaming but was actually living this happiness. All that had almost been shattered, but the future was still theirs. Eve felt good on this birthday as she skipped downstairs to the breakfast table. Ed was again preparing the early morning repast as he had done before his illness. The first thing she saw was a huge red card with the picture of a rose on it. Inside was the sentiment that only husbands and wives could share. Ed took her in his arms and wished her a happy birthday and "I love you so." Eve responded and reassured him in turn of her love for him.

"I'm taking you out to a birthday dinner tonight, to a French restaurant," he told her. When Eve reached her office, she saw several birthday cards on her desk and a handwritten note inviting her to a birthday coffee in her honor that afternoon. She had been aware that her staff had been preparing this party, because by now it had developed into a yearly ritual. She had left her calendar open, and had not scheduled any conferences for the afternoon. She closed her ears to the whispering that was going on outside of her office with Bertha, and pretended not to see the covered cake tins and boxes that were being stored in a corner of the outer office. It was hard to keep her mind on her work. Even though she pretended not to want a party, she would have been mighty disappointed if she had been taken at her word.

The morning finally passed. After lunch Eve became so engrossed in her work that she did not notice how the hours had sped. All of a sudden, there was Bertha at the door to tell Eve that her party was starting, and everyone was waiting for her.

"My gosh, where has the time gone? I forgot all about the party! Look at my hands, they're all dirty, my face must be a shiny mess and my hair flying in all directions. Give me five minutes so I can make myself presentable," Eve exclaimed.

She dashed off to the ladies' room to clean up. Taking a deep breath she walked into the conference room that had been set up for the party. The room was filled with people. To her surprise, she saw Ed. The group burst out in song, "Happy birthday..." after which Eve was ushered to the beautiful table. It had rust-colored chrysanthemums as a centerpiece flanked by candles of the same color. The paper plates, cups and napkins all matched the colors of the centerpiece. Off to one side was a large cake decorated with fancy icing with the words "Happy Birthday, Dr. Hart!"

"How beautiful! Thank you so much! Everything looks so good, how can I choose?" Eve exclaimed. There was a cheery atmosphere of laughter and chatter as people came and went, as they found time from their clinic and office duties. At the height of the party, Jane Johnson requested silence and then, on behalf of the staff, presented a gaily-wrapped package along with a card to Eve. Eve read the card first: "To a Wonderful Boss" and the inside contained the names of all the staff members. Eve handed the card to Ed to be passed around, and then opened the package carefully so as not to tear the ribbons or paper. There was a beautiful sterling silver pin in the shape of an owl perched on a tree limb, with large, sad-looking eyes. Eve burst out, "The wise old owl. Is that me?"

"Not old, just wise," was the chorused reply.

"It's beautiful and I'll love wearing it. Thank you so much," she said as she pinned it onto the lapel of her suit.

As the party wound up, Bertha told Eve, "We're going to wrap up a package of the left-over cookies and cake for you to take home. I'm sure Dr. Wood will enjoy them, if you don't want to eat them. He sure looks good after his long siege of illness." Others had commented on his looks too.

"Oh, I can't take it all. We can't possibly eat that much. Just make a little package and leave something for the others," Eve urged.

"You can always freeze them and use them later," replied Bertha who went about filling the box.

"Thank you for everything. It was a lovely party," Eve called out as she and Ed left. She whispered to him, "They don't know that this is their last birthday party for me." They drove home together since Ed had come downtown by bus. "Just like old times, isn't it?" Ed said as he sat beside Eve in her car.

When they got home Ed told her, "Doll yourself up pretty tonight. We'll make a big evening of it. It's your special day, but it's pretty special for me too. It will be my first night on the town since I was ill."

The hostess directed them to the corner table Ed had reserved. The room had heavy red plush walls, dark red rugs and red upholstered chairs. It had a Victorian look about it. The waitresses also were dressed according to that period. During the rather lengthy wait for their food, they sat back to enjoy the background music and watched other diners being seated.

After a while Eve remarked, "Do you know how one can tell whether or not the couples here tonight are married?"

"No, how do you?"

"Well, just look around you. That young couple over there most assuredly is not married, or at least not very long. Look at the way they are carrying on an animated conversation and see the flirting glances the girl is casting on the young man. Over there is a slightly older couple. The man is very seriously explaining something and the woman is listening intently."

"I'll wager a guess. They are probably having a business conference," Ed said with a laugh.

111

"Maybe you're right! Now those people are certainly married." She pointed surreptitiously to another couple. "The man is yawning his head off and the woman looks bored. They haven't said a word to each other the whole time I've been observing them."

"How do you suppose we look to other people?" Ed wondered.

"I think we have a married look."

"Maybe, but we don't look bored with each other," replied Ed.

"I think what differentiates a married couple from one that is not is they don't have to do their flirting in public. They can be discreet about it because they have the privacy of their own home for their loving," Eve explained.

"That's true and they don't have to try to prove anything either. They already belong to each other," Ed continued in the same vein of thought.

"On the other hand though, the love a happily married couple feels would probably show itself to other people," Eve ventured.

"I'm flirting with you now," Ed teased.

"I think we flirt with each other as much as that young couple, but we don't say much when we are out. Tonight is almost an exception."

Just then their food was set before them interrupting their conversation. They both enjoyed French food so the meal was a treat. After their plates were cleared away, the waitress placed a birthday cake before Eve with a single candle.

"Happy birthday, darling," Ed said quietly as he took a small package from his pocket and gave it to her.

Eve blew out the candle before she opened the package. "How beautiful!" There was a golden pendant with a jade in the center of a Chinese motif on a long golden chain. She hung it around her neck and people at the nearby tables watched the tableau and smiled indulgently.

Ed told Eve, "There are several birthday cards awaiting you at home, and also a small package from your brother."

"That explains it. I wondered that my only brother had forgotten this birthday which is more special than the usual."

"No, he didn't forget. I thought it would be nicer to keep the cards and his present for after we get home," Ed said. After Eve had opened and read the cards, and admired the sterling silver candlesticks she received from her brother, she exclaimed delightedly, "This is one of the nicest birthdays I've ever had. It will be something more to add to my store of memories." She gave Ed a big hug and kiss, as she thanked him for the evening and the lovely present.

CHAPTER SIXTEEN

The next day dawned as another working day. The festivities of yesterday were but memories, but they helped sustain Eve. It was not long before one of the physicians came to tell Eve of her decision. "I talked it over with my husband and we decided I should accept the position if it is offered to me." The others were not interested.

"That's just fine. It would relieve my mind if I could be assured that the programs we've initiated will be continued. In any case, even on an interim basis after I leave, someone will have to take charge until the new person steps in. So I will review with you all current programs and some of my other plans that I won't see to fruition. I'll tell the Health Officer about it."

After telling the Health Officer, Eve set about in a systematic way to review and document each one of the many programs in her department for her successor. It was a tedious job and fatiguing, but necessary for the smooth transfer of responsibilities. She also set about to finish as many things as she could before leaving.

As Eve read past reports, she felt a compelling need to document some of the developments and write a historical summary. After all, she had been the first director of the department. Program after program had been newly initiated or transferred from another department, until she now operated a service program benefiting thousands of patients. The kinds of services had expanded from purely preventive services of keeping babies well, to total medical care for children, expectant mothers and women from poor families, and many, many other services to individuals and other agencies in the community. The department had a booming dental clinic for children. Medical social workers worked with families attending clinics.

"I must be crazy to start writing this historical review, as though I didn't have enough to occupy my time during the remaining weeks," Eve grumbled to Ed.

"I think it's a good idea. So many of your staff joined you only in the last few years. They have no idea of what went on before their time. This would give some continuity to your program," Ed encouraged.

"Things are certainly different today from the way decisions were made some years ago," she said thoughtfully.

"How's that?"

"Earlier, the agency did all the planning and made the decisions. If we wanted to set up another clinic somewhere we investigated the needs and then went there with our services."

"Was that bad?" Ed asked.

"No, not necessarily. It was easier for us to do things that way and things usually got accomplished faster."

"What about now?" Ed asked.

"Changes have occurred in the attitude of patients and groups have been formed to represent the patients. They are no longer satisfied to have decisions made for them. They want a stake in making plans for themselves. You recall the meeting I had months ago with the women regarding referrals for abortions? They dislike a paternalistic attitude toward them," Eve explained.

"Are you able to meet their requests?" Ed asked.

"That's where the difficulty comes. They know what they want," Eve said, "but it takes a long time to convince them and to explain what we can offer in the way of services, and what our limitations are, either legally or financially."

Matters had reached the stage where it was difficult to keep Eve's secret. Bertha wondered at the furious way Eve was going about the files. It was usually Bertha who came to Eve suggesting rearranging files or discarding papers that no longer seemed relevant. Now it was Eve who was methodically going through everything, laying mountains of folders on her desk and filling the wastebaskets. When she was not at the files, she was dictating into the dictaphone summaries from old reports. Every afternoon she closeted herself with her associate behind closed doors. One day Bertha could no longer contain herself, "What's going on here? It looks mighty like a major housecleaning job to me."

"Oh, these files have needed a major overhauling for a long time and I thought now is as good a time as any to tackle them," Eve replied casually.

"It looks like a lot more than that," Bertha muttered as she left the room.

116

The matters with Civil Service could not be held secret much longer either and Eve would have to submit her resignation in writing to make it formal. The time had also come when their home was ready to be put into the hands of a real estate agent. Sooner or later someone from the office would see the ad in the paper. The day had come all too soon for the announcement. Eve had chosen the weekly meeting with her senior staff to tell of her plans. The meeting was scheduled to start promptly at 8:30 A.M., but the same stragglers were late as usual. Without waiting for them, Eve started the meeting. First she informed the group of communications she had received. Before she got through, the late-comers arrived and took their seats. The meeting proceeded as usual, until all topics were exhausted. Just as they were getting ready to leave the conference table, Eve said, "Will you please stay for another moment. I have an announcement to make."

Everybody sat down again with expectant looks. Eve started with an explanation. "As you know, my husband was very ill this past summer and I almost lost him. His recuperation has been slow but steady. When you saw him a short time ago, he looked quite well."

"Has he had a relapse?" someone asked.

"No, and I wish I could tell you that things are just fine now," she replied.

"Are there complications then?"

"No, not really," Eve replied slowly.

The group began to fidget, waiting for her to speak. But before their thoughts went too far afield, she continued, "We're very fortunate that my husband has completely recovered, but it has been necessary for him to curtail his usual activities. Increasingly, it has become more and more difficult for him to stand our severe winters, quite apart from his recent illness. The illness of course made things worse."

"Are you telling us now that you will be taking your usual winter vacation early for Dr. Wood to recuperate faster?"

"I'm afraid it's more than that," Eve said softly. "I mean that we will have to move permanently to a warmer climate. I have just submitted my resignation to take effect in six weeks."

Shocked looks met Eve, with exclamations of "Oh, no!" and "You can't mean it."

117

Eve, with emotion in her voice, said, "It isn't easy for me, either. I've agonized over my decision. I'd give anything if I could continue as before. I love my work so and associating with all of you. But now my first responsibility is to my husband. He needs me, and I must accompany him so he can have a chance to live his life in reasonable health and comfort. We must get away from here, from the cold and its problems."

"What will happen here?" was the next question.

"I've made plans for that. If everything goes as planned, and I don't see anything to the contrary, continuity will be preserved."

The suspense was hard to contain. They wanted to know what those plans were. This did not hold true for everyone. There were several who had not said a word since Eve's announcement, but sat in stunned silence staring at her, others with downcast eyes, as though hiding their tears.

"I am working on a smooth transfer to my successor. Civil Service will see that the best qualified person takes over. The job might even be promotional within the agency."

All eyes turned to the other physicians who had sat quietly listening.

Eve rose to terminate the discussion. "I wish you would tell your staffs. I feel very badly about this, just as I see you do. There is nothing else I can do about it," and she left the room. When she got to her office she summoned Bertha and told her everything she had just told her senior staff. Without waiting for her response, Eve left for lunch.

She sat again in the corner of the busy cafeteria as she had so many times before. She was extremely sad and felt very lonely. The past had receded and there was no future. She was drifting in nothingness.

When she got back to her office she saw that the news had spread. The office areas were very quiet as she walked through. Eyes were downcast. As she passed the desk of one of her favorite clerks she heard a soft, tearful voice saying, "Who's going to take my side now?"

Eve stopped and asked in a surprised voice, "What do you mean? Have I ever taken your side?"

"Yes, you have."

Then Eve understood. This clerk had potential, and Eve directed her into a promotional job where she could use her

118

skills. This had meant establishing a new job category in the department. There was a further bond between then. They shared a common birthday and had gotten into the habit of exchanging birthday cards. Eve was really fond of this attractive and bright girl.

Eve went to her desk but found it hard to concentrate. Several of her staff came in to say how sorry they were. They also seemed anxious about their own situations.

Eve assured them that everything would turn out fine, and that the programs would continue uninterrupted. "That isn't what I mean," was one reply. "The working conditions will not be the same. The morale has usually been so good around here. I feel I have always been able to come to you when I had problems."

"I'm sure that will continue. I would think my successor would have an open door policy too. It's not unique with me, you know."

Bertha told Eve, "This explains everything, your snooping in the files and your non-stop dictating."

"I'll miss your snide remarks and nastiness," was Eve's joshing reply.

"What do you want me to do? Weep crocodile tears? No, to be serious I'll miss you like anything, but I'll save my tears until I'm alone tonight, and can shed them in privacy." The atmosphere in the office was heavy with unshed tears. Eve could take it no longer. She told Bertha, "I can't stand it here. I'm going home to shed my own tears." She thought, as she drove home in tears, "It's something to find out during your lifetime that you're appreciated and loved. Usually the person is already dead by the time the accolades come."

Ed was surprised to see her home so early. "I couldn't stand it any longer. I was crying and so were many others. I couldn't concentrate on my work, so I came home."

"I've been thinking about you all day and wondering how things would go. Was it hard for you to tell them?" Ed asked with compassion.

"The telling wasn't so hard, but when I got back from lunch, everybody in the department knew about it, and then it was a pretty bleak atmosphere," Eve choked.

Ed took her in his arms and she sobbed against his shoulder. "Everything will turn out all right for us. You just wait and see," he comforted her.

"I hope so, but it's so hard now," Eve said as she swallowed a sob.

During the evening the tremendous showing of affection by many of her staff was reinforced when one of her consultants telephoned to tell Eve, "I had to call you and tell you how much I will miss you, and to thank you for all your help, so I could grow in my job. I thought if I didn't gather the courage to tell you now and thank you, I might not do it later."

"I appreciate your telling me. It makes it easier for me to accept my own decision, when I know all my efforts were not in vain," Eve answered quietly and calmly.

A humble and thankful, though tearful Eve, went to bed that night with peace in her heart.

CHAPTER SEVENTEEN

The days went by. One day Eve looked forward eagerly to the move. On another she wasn't so sanguine.

Eve had her associate sit in on all the conferences she held with her own staff, with others in the agency and with outside persons, if these meetings reflected in any way on the department's program. One by one, the red tape was being cleared. The staff had settled down and seemed ready to accept her leaving.

Eve joked with them, "Don't be too sure I'll step down. Although I've submitted my resignation, I have more than a month on the job yet, and I might just change my mind."

She was countered with, "That would be just fine with us. We don't want you to leave!"

So the days went on, without a dull moment. On some days Eve had misgivings. Would she and Ed be able to adjust to yet another place which was different from any they had ever lived in before? Could they make new friends in a strange environment this late in life? On these days, it seemed she could not get anything done. There was an ache inside that would not let up. The weather was not helping any either. The mornings dawned grey and overcast. The wind whipped the trees bare of their remaining leaves.

"Any day now we'll have our first snow," Eve told Ed one morning. "This place has hot, long summers for half the year and for the other half just as long cold, cold winters."

"Then you should enjoy the long springs and beautiful falls where we are going. The winters there will be very short and very mild," he consoled.

"I guess so," was her reply. By the time Eve got out on the park road, it started to rain. Her already miserable mood became even more depressed. She hated the idea of leaving, yet at the same time she was looking forward to moving to a new home in the sunny, warm climate.

The office felt chilly so Eve put on the sweater she kept in her closet for just such days as this. After a while, she realized that this was one of the days when there would be no heat at all, because repairs were being done on the heating apparatus. This usually occurred each fall, but why it had to happen on a day like this was beyond her comprehension. The next morning at breakfast, Ed had a very croaky voice. Eve advised him to stay indoors. That evening she too complained of a sore throat. The next morning Ed had a moderately high fever.

"Oh, not again! You can't get the same thing all over again. You're not on any drugs even," Eve moaned.

"How's your throat?" Ed asked.

"It still feels rough, but I don't have a fever."

"It must be the flu. The symptoms all point to that. Too bad we didn't take our flu vaccine yet. We didn't expect to be exposed to it this early in the season," Ed said.

"You stay in bed, so you won't develop any complications," Eve admonished.

Since she had no fever she continued to go to work each day but came home at noon to prepare food for Ed and to see how he was faring. He spent his time reading and sleeping. With each succeeding day his fever was a bit lower until by Friday it was almost normal. But by noon on the same Friday, Eve felt chilly and her head was beginning to feel light. She continued at the office, and thought to herself, "It's a good thing tomorrow is Saturday. I have the entire weekend to rest. Maybe I'll feel O.K. by Monday."

On the way home, she stopped at the supermarket to stock up on food supplies. She was having definite chills.

"I better get home soon," she thought as she rushed on with her shopping.

She put the foods away when she arrived home and only then did she tell Ed that she was not feeling well. At his urging she took her temperature, which was considerably above normal. Only then did she give up and go to bed.

"It's my turn to take care of you now," Ed told her as he got out of bed to put more blankets over Eve who was shivering with the cold.

"What's going to happen to us?" she cried. "We've never been sick at the same time. You're not well enough to be up and doing things. You'll only have a relapse," she panicked.

"Just relax, nothing will happen to me," he reassured her. "I'm not going to do any more than I have to. I'll only get up to put the food on a tray. And it's no big deal to put the dishes into the dishwasher. Let's take one day at a time."

That night Eve tossed and turned. She had a splitting headache and her nose was so stuffy she had trouble breathing. At short intervals she was troubled with a dry hacking cough. Her chills had subsided, but now she was so hot, she felt like throwing off the covers. Ed prepared a hot drink and set up a steaming apparatus which stopped her coughing and eventually she fell asleep.

In the morning, Ed popped thermometers into both mouths. His temperature was normal for the first time, but Eve's was higher than before. Ed had been a perfectly good patient, but Eve was very impatient. She complained and continued tossing and turning. She was perspiring one moment and feeling cold the next. Her head also continued to throb. She was so restless that finally in exasperation Ed said, "Why don't you stop fighting it. It won't make you better any faster. In fact it might slow your recovery."

"I feel so miserable and my head is aching so," Eve complained.

They got through the day eventually. Ed's temperature continued normal and Eve's started to go down too, although it took four days before it showed normal. By the next day her headache had subsided and she slept quietly almost the entire day except when her coughing bothered her.

"See, I'm not fighting anymore. It's only that I had this terrible headache. Don't you think I'm a pretty good patient now?" Eve asked in a childish sort of way. She stayed home all that week. "Of all times to get ill! Just when we have so much to do. Do you think we can still hold on to our timetable?" She was determined not to let her illness interfere with the date they had selected for their departure.

The following Monday when Eve returned to work completely recovered, Bertha came to her saying, "The staff wants to have a farewell party for you and Dr. Wood, and we would like to select the date most convenient for you."

"Oh, no, we don't want any party," was Eve's first reaction.

Bertha countered with, "You'll have to let us do this for you. We'd be terribly disappointed if we couldn't." Bertha convinced her that she would be depriving her staff of the opportunity of saying, "Thank you," and they would indeed be very disappointed if she refused to let them have the farewell party. Eve finally gave in, but added, "O.K. But don't overdo it. Make it simple."

One Sunday evening the real estate agent called, telling them there was a prospective buyer who wanted to submit an offer for their property that very evening. It was late but the agent stressed, "It should not be delayed, it should be decided right now when the irons are hot." So the deal was made, with the buyer agreeing to permit Eve and Ed to stay in the house until near the end of the year.

This started a flurry of activity. Their home began to look very desolate and bare. They disposed of many items they did not wish to take along. Their last two weeks in the city would be spent in a motel. At least Ed would spend his days there. Fortunately, Eve still had her office to go to. She was finishing her tasks with no time to spare, but none to waste, either.

The Christmas holidays came and went with no special festivities arranged by Eve and Ed. Roy and Kay invited them for Christmas Day. Eve and Ed had their sons over for a final dinner in a bleak and stripped-down house.

The day arrived when the movers came to pack, returning the next day to load the van. They were about finished when Eve came home. After they had left, Eve and Ed stood in the empty rooms where they had spent so many happy years. Eve laid her head on Ed's shoulder and sobbed. He was not far from tears himself. For the last time they closed the door to their cherished home to drive to the motel.

CHAPTER EIGHTEEN

Things were easing off at the office for Eve. She was becoming more and more detached from the crisis situations as well as the everyday problems. Her thoughts were in the future. A party atmosphere began to prevade the offices. There was much coming and going at Bertha's desk. There were mysterious lists that had nothing to do with department business. The date for the farewell party was set for Thursday evening, just prior to Eve's last day.

Eve and Ed were caught up in a round of activities during their last two weeks. They never imagined they had so many friends who were sorry to see them go. They had one invitation after another. Their social club had an open house for them on a cold, snowy Sunday afternoon, at the home of one of the members. On the last remaining Sunday there was a brunch for them at a beautiful private club, hosted by a service organization to which Eve had belonged for many years. Ed's former staff also held a farewell party. There was much talk at these more intimate parties about the future plans of the others. The days of retirement were not too far away for some of them. The self-employed were adamant that they certainly would never retire. Those who would face compulsory retirement were divided as to whether they would look for a new home somewhere else, just as Eve and Ed were doing, or whether it would be impossible for them to leave family and friends. One said, "Our children visit us so seldom even now, when we're in the same city, that it wouldn't make much difference to us. We'd probably see them just as often if we lived farther away."

"And when they visited you, you'd have their undivided attention for a few days at least," interjected another.

"Yes, you can't live your life through that of your children. You must live your own life whether you like it or not," Eve noted.

Ed was holding up remarkably well during all the parties and socializing. One day however, when Eve met him at a club for lunch with still another friend, he didn't seem as spry as he had been, and Eve was worried. Ed whispered to her when their host was busy with the hostess that he felt very dizzy. He was once again completely withdrawn, and was not making much effort to talk.

How would he ever get safely back to the motel? They had driven over in separate cars. She prayed silently to herself, "Please keep him well. Please make it possible that we can leave this place together for our new home." Eve was scared they might never make it there. It seemed such a long time ago that she had made her decision to leave, and here they were, still in the north country in the middle of the winter. Eve followed Ed in her car as he slowly drove back to the motel. "What's wrong with you now?" she asked with apprehension, after they arrived. But the trouble cleared up in a couple of days. "I have to be careful not to turn my head suddenly in this direction," Ed demonstrated, "but otherwise, I seem to be all right."

"You better make an appointment to see your doctor one more time before we leave. We won't be able to arrange for a physician immediately in the new place," Eve told him.

So together then went to the doctor, a few days later. She sat in the waiting room with flushed face, while Ed was being seen. The feeling Eve experienced was close to apprehension and her heart beat faster.

In order to pass the time, Eve started to examine the furnishings in the waiting room aimlessly. Her reverie was broken by the conversation of the women seated near her. They spoke of their aches and pains in great detail. Then they went on to describe the operations of their relatives. Eve wondered what was going on with Ed and the doctor. Just at that moment she saw Ed coming out of the examining room accompanied by the doctor who was telling Ed, "Take care of yourself now, and enjoy your retirement in the great southwest."

Ed had a grin on his face. "What did he find?" was Eve's first question.

"Nothing serious, just an old ear problem which troubles me from time to time."

"Then there is nothing to keep us from leaving," Eve said with relief.

"Where did you ever get such an idea, that there would be?" Ed asked. "I've been keeping my fingers crossed that nothing more would happen to us to cancel our moving."

It would soon be over. On the last evening of their stay at the motel Eve found Ed in the midst of packing when she arrived. He had laid out his clothes on the two beds, and had placed other articles on every free surface there was in the room.

"My gosh, what in the world are you doing?" Eve exclaimed as she came in. "I was afraid you might get here before I was finished. All my things are so mixed up I thought I would rearrange them and repack them in the suitcases," replied Ed.

"O.K., O.K. I won't disturb you. Just clear out a space for me on my bed so I can lie down for a moment before the big party tonight. I came home early so I could rest a while."

Ed moved over his things on the bed and Eve lay down turning her back to Ed and his activities. She must have dozed off because when she came to, it was dusk. She got up yawning and stretching.

"That felt good. I think I'll leave my final packing until we get back tonight. I don't have too much to do, except for the things in the kitchenette. We have only enough food for our breakfast tomorrow morning and the staples we'll be taking along. I'll probably be so excited after the party tonight, I'll need something to keep me busy for a while so I can fall asleep."

She went off for a bath and to dress. "You better get ready too," she called to Ed.

"You look like my bride," Ed complimented Eve when she was ready.

"You look mighty handsome too," she told him.

The skies had cleared, the stars were shining and there was a crescent of a new moon overhead. They stood for a moment admiring the view. But it was bitterly cold so they got into the car to drive to the party. They were met at the door of the private club by two physicians in Eve's department, one of whom pinned a corsage on Eve's gown and gave Ed a boutonniere for his lapel. They were directed to a place in the center of the reception area to greet the guests as they arrived. The unofficial photographer of the agency placed himself next to Eve and Ed to take pictures of them with each new group of arrivals.

To her pleasant surprise, there were several of Eve's former staff who had come to honor her and to bid her

127

farewell. There were some she had not seen since they had left the department. It was good to see them. The same was happening to Ed who was enthusiastically greeting former colleagues and associates. He introduced her to those she was not acquainted with. One man congratulated Ed and said, "I hadn't heard that you got married."

Eve whispered to Ed after the man had left them, "My gosh, he thinks we're newlyweds. You better correct him later when you get a chance to talk to him again."

"That's what happens. How would he have known all these years that Dr. Hart was also Mrs. Wood?" The place was becoming more and more crowded as ever more guests arrived. Eve was especially happy when she saw an old friend who had been in the same service club with her some years ago and who was prominent in her own right. Her husband accompanied her. He told Eve, "I don't usually go to the many events my wife has to attend, but I came tonight because she is so fond of you and I too wanted to honor this occasion for you." "We're very grateful you did," Eve replied.

At last they left the official greeting line to mingle with the guests. Eve tried to steer the persons from outside the agency, who seemed a bit lost among the crowd, to other people whom she thought would be compatible with them. Besides their own former staff there were retired persons from other departments of the agency, including a former boss of Eve's and his wife. It was strange how little some of them had changed over the years. In fact a few looked definitely younger than they had in their working years. Eve was moved to exclaim, "Retirement must certainly agree with you. You look so well and so young."

"Welcome to our ranks. It's a wonderful state of life and we hope you will enjoy it as much as we do."

"I hope so. It's good to hear something good about retirement. You should know, having enjoyed and lived it for a while now," Eve replied in a tone of voice that seemed to indicate that she didn't quite believe it yet. When it seemed there was no more room to turn around, and everybody had drunk as much punch as he wanted, the call came to line up for the buffet dinner in the adjoining room, with Eve and Ed at the head of the line. They had places of honor at the head table, flanked on both sides by guests who included the master of ceremonies and his wife. Then came the traditional speeches. Ed had placed a tape recorder under the podium. He wanted to catch all the words that were said so he could listen to them again at a later time. With his decreased hearing ability he was sure he would miss some of the finer points of the talks in his excitement. The speeches, fortunately, were few and short. They included the presentation of merit awards to Eve and Ed from the city.

Then came the time for the gifts. They were lovely indeed. Eve and Ed thanked everybody for coming, for the beautiful gifts which they would always cherish, and especially they thanked those who had arranged the wonderful evening. The party was over, but people were reluctant to leave. They came up to the head table one by one to bid good-by to Eve and Ed who were standing behind their chairs, and to wish them well in the days to come. There were tears in the eyes of some of the women as they shook hands or embraced Eve in a farewell gesture.

They were back in their motel room. As Eve had predicted, she was indeed too excited to go to bed immediately. Together they rehashed the events of the evening, admired their gifts and played the tape recorder. "That sounds funny," Eve grimaced, "I even made a grammatical error. I hope nobody noticed it."

"Never mind, it sounded O.K. and it went over well," Ed replied.

"You sure praised your girls, but didn't say much of anything about your other staff," Eve teased Ed.

"The professionals always get credit for everything, so I wanted to do this for the clerks who are always in the background and work every bit as hard as the others, but are never applauded for their contribution," was Ed's reply.

Eve was busily doing the last of her packing, so that by the time she was finished she had quieted down and was able to go to bed. "I'm not going to get up very early. They can't fire or reprimand me anymore if I am late to the office. I really don't know what I'll be doing there anyway. I wouldn't even go down, it's sort of an anticlimax, except it's supposed to be my last working day," Eve said before falling asleep. The next morning they ate the last of their victuals and Eve left Ed to wash up in the kitchen as she got ready to go for the last time to her office. It was mid-morning when she sauntered leisurely in. Already she was a stranger there. The staff was busily at work. She felt like a visitor, which she in fact was. But there was still a program for her. The department was having yet another farewell party for her, complete with coffee and cakes and even another gift!

"Some of the staff couldn't get to the party last night because of their evening clinic commitments and they felt awfully bad about it and so we thought we would do this," Bertha explained.

Eve sat with her coffee cup as one after another of her staff came in. There were thank-yous on all sides, final good-bys and more tears. Eve made one last search through her desk to see if she had forgotten anything personal. She handed over the keys to her private files to Bertha who would give them to her successor. Then she gathered her remaining things, waved as she walked through the door for the last time. There was a lump in her throat at the finality of it all. She would have lunch downtown before she drove to the motel to join Ed. For the last time she went to her familiar cafeteria. Again she sat alone with her thoughts, surrounded by the din of voices. There was no tenseness in her now, no more unsolved problems to handle. There was just sadness that it was all over, that another phase in her life was ended. Abruptly Eve turned these morbid thoughts aside. A new phase was starting in her life and she began to feel excitement at the prospect. It was not the end of things, but a new beginning for Ed and her. Only time would tell what adventures and happiness it would bring to them. Eve was all smiles as she greeted Ed at the door to the motel room. Swiftly they packed the remaining things into the trunk of the car. Their household furnishings and Ed's car had been shipped. He had already paid for the motel room. All the farewells had been said. There was nothing else to keep them there any longer.

Ed took Eve into his arms and said, "We're going to continue to have a wonderful life together, darling. You just see."

"I'm sure we will," murmured Eve.

They got into the car. The sun was high, but already on its way to the west. It would arrive there ahead of them and welcome them to their new home. There was only joy and hope for the future in their hearts now, and anticipation, as they began the long drive to the new life they would happily share together.